Using Poetry
to Teach Reading
and Language Arts

A HANDBOOK FOR
ELEMENTARY SCHOOL TEACHERS

Using Poetry to Teach Reading and Language Arts

A HANDBOOK FOR ELEMENTARY SCHOOL TEACHERS

RICHARD J. SMITH

University of Wisconsin-Madison

TEACHERS COLLEGE PRESS

Teachers College, Columbia University
New York and London

Published by Teachers College Press, 1234 Amsterdam Avenue, New York, N.Y. 10027

Library of Congress Cataloging in Publication Data

Smith, Richard John, 1930–
    Using poetry to teach reading and language arts.

    Includes index.
    1. Language arts (Elementary) 2. Poetry—Study and teaching (Elementary) I. Title.
LB1576.S628 1984   372.6   84–8682

ISBN 0-8077-2708-3

Manufactured in the United States of America

90 89 88 87 86 85   1 2 3 4 5 6

Contents

Preface

This book was written to help elementary school teachers discover the power of poetry for teaching reading and the other language arts. The title reflects the fact that in many schools reading and language arts are separate curricula.

When I was teaching reading and language arts, I often discussed the form and content of poems. My primary, perhaps only, objective was appreciation. For the past few years I have been experimenting with poems as vehicles for other instructional objectives of the reading and language arts curricula. The positive results of my experimenting encouraged me to enlist the assistance of other teachers in further experiments with classroom instruction focused on a variety of specific reading and language arts objectives using poetry as instructional material. The enthusiastic responses of those teachers and their students provided the motivation and much of the content for this book.

The book is divided into five chapters. All five are intended to be highly practical for prospective and practicing teachers in grades one through six. The discussions in the first three chapters focus on the why of using poetry for language arts instruction and offer a number of suggestions for teaching language arts so that a variety of specific objectives are met. Taken as a whole, the first three chapters might be considered the explication of a theory for using poetry to attain specific objectives of the elementary school reading and language arts curricula.

Chapters four and five are unlike chapters in other teaching methods textbooks in that they consist of poems I wrote for students and lesson plans for teaching them. Those in chapter four seem most appropriate for students in grades one through three, and those in chapter five seem most appropriate for students in grades four through six. However, teachers may make other decisions about the grades for which they are most appropriate. All the poems were written with students, teachers, and specific reading and language arts curriculum objectives in mind. Before inclusion in this book, they were all tested with elementary students for their age-group appeal as well as for their potential for skills development. All received high grades on both counts.

As readers of this book you are invited to select the poems in chapters four and five you think would enrich your instructional program. Immediately following each poem is a brief description "About the Poem" and a complete plan for teaching it. The poems may be duplicated and circulated to the students for classroom use.

I have made it a point to visit the classrooms of students and teachers who have used the poems in this book to answer any questions they might like to ask about the poems. I always come away feeling that they have enjoyed them, so I am quite certain your students will, too. I also find they are interested in the person who wrote the poems. Since your students may also be interested in the poet as well as the poems, I offer the following transcript of one of my visits to a fourth grade classroom.

Question: Are you a teacher?
Answer: Yes.
Question: What grade do you teach?
Answer: I teach at the university now, but I used to teach high school and elementary school students.
Question: When do you write your poems?
Answer: Mostly on weekends and real early in the morning. Sunday morning is a good time for me.
Question: How do you know what to write about? I mean, like that caterpillar one.
Answer: Well, I saw that caterpillar crossing a country road near my cabin and I thought, "Wow, he's really brave."
Question: Where's your cabin?
Answer: In central Wisconsin, about a hundred miles north of Madison.
Question: Why do you like to write poems?
Answer: Because they sound good in my head. And I never know where one is going to end when I start it. It's like playing a game.
Question: How long does it take you to write a poem?
Answer: My poems are all pretty short, so not long. Never more than an hour for the first draft of one. Of course, I may have to patch it up, make it better, for a day or two. Maybe even a week or a month. But if it takes longer than an hour to get it down in the first place—forget it.
Question: How can you rhyme words so good?
Answer: I wrote a poem about that:

My head is full of words that rhyme;
They pop right out most any time.
I take a pen at school or home,
And, wham! I go and write a poem.
Oh, my gosh, look what I've done.
I've written down another one.

Question: A lot of your poems are about nature. Do you like nature?
Answer: Yes, I do. I spend all the time I can outdoors. I like to hike,
     canoe, swim, watch animals, and stuff like that.
Question: Are you going to write some more poems?
Answer: I hope so. If I do, do you want to read them?
Question: Do we have to write about them?

Acknowledgments

I am thankful to many people who assisted in one way or another with the preparation of this book. Chief among them are Velma Dauer, Colleen Larson, and Dale Wortley, all reading/language arts specialists and doctoral candidates at the University of Wisconsin–Madison when this book was conceived and written. They encouraged, guided, and edited my efforts throughout the preparation of the manuscript.

I am also thankful to the many classroom teachers and their students who helped me prove that poetry is an excellent literary form for reading and language arts instruction in the elementary grades. They were also helpful in testing my original poems and guiding my efforts to write the kind of verse children enjoy and can use for skills development.

Grateful acknowledgment is made for permission to reprint the following material:

The poems "Behind My Smile," "Once I Did," "Outside My Tent," and "What Happened?" from Richard J. Smith, "Poetry and Reading Skills," *Instructor* (May 1983).

The poems "The Bravest Thing I Know," "Don't Catch the Flu," "Geraldine Jackson," "Imagining by the Sea," "My Dreams," and "My Scary Book" from James F. Baumann and Dale D. Johnson, eds., *Reading Instruction and the Beginning Teacher: A Practical Guide* (Minneapolis: Burgess Publishing Company, 1984).

"Caution" from pamphlet published by the State of Michigan Department of National Resources.

Using Poetry to Teach Reading and Language Arts

A HANDBOOK FOR ELEMENTARY SCHOOL TEACHERS

CHAPTER 1

Using Poetry in Reading
and Language Arts Instruction

The value of using poetry for attaining a variety of reading and language arts curriculum objectives is not nearly as difficult to explain as the fact that it typically has been used so sparingly for that purpose. For any number of reasons, carefully selected poetry has as good, if not better, potential for reading, writing, speaking, and listening skills development than the expository paragraphs and narratives that comprise the bulk of anthologies, kits, workbooks, and other development materials that are typically used for basic instruction in reading and language arts. In addition, poetry has great potential for teaching creative thinking, mental imagery, and other less basic objectives of reading and language arts curricula.

Perhaps developers of reading and language arts curricula and teachers have overlooked poems as major instructional vehicles because they have stereotyped them as fragile creations, not structurally strong enough for basic instruction. Poems are often presented to children as if they must be mouthed gently and touched only by questions of appreciation: "Did you like this poem?" "Tell us why you liked it." Stewig (1980) observes that "too often students think of poems as delicate images of beautiful, fragile things, encompassed in a sunlit or moonlit world where little action takes place" (p. 230). The art work that accompanies many poems in instructional materials and children's magazines furthers the stereotype by dressing them in gossamer and lace. Who would dare to pull apart or dig into such a lovely thing? And material used for instructional purposes must be dug into, at least a little.

This stereotypic view of poetry and what it implies for language arts instruction are wrong. Poems can be discussed, analyzed, and used for specific skills instruction. They can, indeed, be given to children for instructional purposes without fear of damage and without fear that students will develop a distaste for poetry. My experience has been that students' appreciation of poetry is likely to be enhanced rather than

1

diminished by typical instructional activities such as identifying main ideas, discussing the content, using context clues or phonics analysis to identify unfamiliar words, reading orally with good expression, or writing paraphrases of key ideas.

Rarely are poems found in elementary school teachers' lesson plans as material for skills development. Rarely are poems taught with specific instructional objectives in mind. Elementary school teachers have not tapped the great reservoir of instructional possibilities inherent in poetry.

Wolsch and Wolsch (1982) comment that "working with words is a craft, like shaping clay. Word crafters speak of their pleasures and their pain. They work with heightened language; they laugh, they cry, they dance with words" (p. 1). No writer crafts words more precisely, more descriptively, or with more insight into people and their environments than the poet. The messages of poets speak of pleasure and pain with heightened language. Their words laugh and dance and cry. Therefore, poems are excellent language models for children. To learn communication skills with poetry is to learn with language at its best. Burns and Broman (1983) suggest that "if teachers would read a good poem to children every day, the essential elements of rich language use (form, rhythm, words, and subject matter) might be more quickly acquired by the children" (p. 397).

TYPES OF POEMS

Poems That Rhyme

While rhyme is not an essential characteristic of poetry, many poems rhyme; those that do are excellent sources for helping students learn to use context clues, an important comprehension and vocabulary development strategy. Smith (1978, p. 15) talks about the "reduction of uncertainty" as readers process a message. The farther into a word, sentence, paragraph (stanza), or whole selection the listener or reader gets the more predictable the remainder becomes. Listening "ahead" or reading "ahead" improves comprehension. The listening or reading ahead process is enhanced when the message rhymes. Notice the ease with which the deleted word from each stanza in the following poem can be replaced because of the assistance provided by the rhyme scheme.[1]

---

[1]All the poems in this chapter were written by the author and appear in either chapter four or chapter five with lesson plans for teaching them.

GERALDINE JACKSON

For a kid who loves to eat
Geraldine Jackson can't be beat.
All considered, bite for bite,
She has a monstrous _____.
Smack!

She always, always cleans her plate.
For dinner time she's never late.
Neither her mother nor her pop
Ever tell her, "Time to _____."
Burp!

Once she ate three lemon pies.
I don't know how she closed her eyes.
Drank a milk shake so darn thick
Even Geraldine got _____.
Ugh!

I saw her eat a whole fried chicken,
And then she even got to lickin'
Off the bones 'til they were bare.
Wouldn't you think her clothes would _____?
Rip!

Geraldine just makes me cry.
Yes, I cry. Do you know why?
Geraldine can eat like that
And never gain an ounce of _____.
Sob!

Periodic practice using context clues to replace deleted words in poems is good training for students who need instruction in context clue analysis and for students whose comprehension skills need strengthening. The rhyming aspect of the poems contributes to the students' sense of reading as a meaning-getting process and thereby facilitates fluent oral reading as well.

Poems with Rhythm

Rhythm is another characteristic of many poems written for children. Not only do children have positive affective responses to poems that have rhythm (they enjoy the "feel" of the rhythm), but they also find it easier to read material with a strong rhythm than material without. I have observed many students struggle with the oral reading of a poem until they fall into the rhythm implanted by the author. Then their reading takes on an expressiveness unmatched by their reading of free verse or prose. I have also observed students achieve a higher level of listening and reading comprehension with rhythmic poetry, an achievement I attribute to the meaning cues in the intonation patterns of rhythmic poems. Poems with strong rhythm are also excellent for choral speaking experiences. In this regard Kean and Personke (1976) advise teachers of young children to "select verses with strong cadence or rhythm. Rhythmic expression is one of the earliest oral interpretative skills for children to grasp. A steady, strong rhythm is a good beginning and is also an aid to memorization" (p. 123).

Compare the ease of reading (orally or silently) two versions of "Don't Catch the Flu."

DON'T CATCH THE FLU (VERSION ONE)

Shivering is what you'll do
If you should go and catch the flu.
And you'll be hot and thirsty, too,
If you should go and catch the flu.

Throwing up is what you'll do
If you should go and catch the flu.
And you'll be dizzy, shaky, too,
If you should go and catch the flu.

It's terrible the things you'll do
If you should go and catch the flu.
And what I say I know is true,
'Cause I just went and caught the flu.

DON'T CATCH THE FLU (VERSION TWO)

If you should catch the flu, you would shiver.
You would also be hot and thirsty.
Catching the flu would also cause you to throw up.
Dizziness and shakiness are other symptoms of the flu.
Catching the flu is a terrible thing.
I know it is because I caught it.

Students who find prose passages difficult to appreciate or understand are often pleasantly surprised to discover that the content in rhythmic poems comes to them smoothly and clearly. The fluent reading experiences children have with poems can be effective in providing an essential base for fluent prose reading.

Short Poems

Another characteristic of children's poems that offers good potential for reading and language arts instruction is their brevity. Children love to reach closure on just about everything in their lives. One characteristic of childhood is the inability to wait for anything. In certain poems the entire story is told in a few lines:

SYMPATHY

A truck rolled by, its load piled high.
"My tires hurt," it pouted.
I limped along, my own song gone.
"You're not alone!" I shouted.

The length of a literary selection is a factor in student fatigue. Short, complete selections allow students to retain some physical and emotional energy for post-reading or listening discussions and other literature-related activities. Students' motivation to write or talk about a literary selection is often diminished after a too-long reading or listening experience. A short, carefully chosen poem can be the starting point for highly motivated speaking and writing experiences that give students the practice they need in expressing their own ideas.

Ridiculous and Humorous Poems

Delight in the ridiculous is another characteristic of childhood that can be satisfied by the poet faster, and perhaps better, than by writers of any other genre:

CAN YOU IMAGINE?

Can you imagine:
A goose reading a newspaper?
Two dogs riding bicycles?
Three ducks wearing raincoats?
Four monkeys shaving?
Five elephants dancing?
Six birds playing with a cat?
Seven rabbits climbing trees?
Eight camels fishing?
I can't!

DUCK WALK

Nothing's slicker than a duck
Afloat upon the water.
But when it walks along the shore,
It really shouldn't oughter.

Ridiculousness is a feature of one type of children's poetry that delights readers and listeners. It also frees children's imaginations for writing their own ridiculous thoughts. Pilon (1978) says, "Children should be encouraged to make up their own nonsense verses, coin words, and use poetic license, just as the authors they have been listening to have felt free to do" (p. 106).

Children prefer humor to pathos in literature. Humorous children's poems are abundant. I have never had to look far to find humorous poems for elementary students.

The element of humor in a poem can do much to help students develop positive attitudes toward poetry, and certainly this is an important, often unreached, objective of reading and language arts curricula.

Poems About Children's Feelings

Children love to find themselves in literary characters. For that matter, so do adults. Why else a Charlie Brown? Certainly, vicarious experience is enjoyable, and extending children's lives through literature is an important curricular objective. However, that journey from self to others starts with self, and poems are often better mirrors of feelings than prose selections. Poems invite empathy more openly than other literary forms because, for the most part, poets open themselves to their readers more explicitly than other writers. The following poem has pleased many elementary students because it expresses a life experience they recognize as one of their own.

BEHIND MY SMILE

If you think I'm never sad,
I'll tell you what let's do.
You be me for just one day,
And I'll in turn be you.

You just hop inside of me,
And be me for awhile.
Think my thoughts, and do my jobs;
Find out what makes me smile.

By the way, while you are me
As one day passes by,
You'll also learn behind my smile
I sometimes want to cry.

Obviously, literature that students understand and can empathize with is a good launching pad for the development of reading, writing, speaking, and listening skills. It stimulates students' feelings and encourages them to express those feelings.

Poems That Promote Thoughtfulness

I asked a third grader in a school I visited if she would rather read a story or a poem, a question I occasionally ask elementary students because of my special interest in children's poetry. Unexpectedly, since many children have more positive feelings toward stories than poems, she said, "a poem." I asked why, and she explained, "Because poems are more fun to discuss." This response surprised me even more than her answer to my first question and prompted me to observe more carefully elementary teachers' post-reading discussions of stories compared to their discussions of poems. There was a difference.

The teachers I observed were much more mechanical and more closely tied to the teacher's manual when they led discussions about stories in their basal series than they were with poems. In questioning students about stories, teachers were searching for the correct answers, always testing students' recall of what happened in the story. In discussing poems they asked more open-ended questions above the cognitive level of literal comprehension. The students became more thoughtful and more personally involved with poems than with stories.

A major difference I noticed in my observations was that students' responses to stories appeared to be much more predictable than their responses to poems. There is a sameness about the stories in basal readers that promotes mechanical rather than thoughtful responses. Bates (1981) explains that "recent theorists have suggested that stories have an underlying structure which can be described in terms of a generalized organizational structure. People learn this organizational pattern or 'story schema' and expect a story to follow it" (p. 4). Clearly, students may develop schemata or expectations for stories that can detract from thoughtful reading and may, in fact, encourage superficial reading. They can develop the bad habit of reading only for plots and become bored because of the predictability of those plots. The same is not so true of poems. Poems are usually reflections of an author's unusual or unpredictable thoughts and, therefore, require careful reading. The following is a good example.

My Dreams

Sometimes my dreams are very merry;
Other times they're very scary.
I've danced at balls with queens and kings,
Been chased and caught by monstrous things.

Where am I when I'm asleep?
I know my body's snuggled deep
Beneath the covers on my bed.
But where's the inside of my head?

Do my thoughts go out walking
When I stop my daytime talking?
Do they visit strange new places?
See different lands and different faces?

I think that they don't stay at home,
For in my dreams I often roam
Through areas unknown to me—
I've climbed a mountain, sailed a sea.

I never dream that I'm asleep,
Under covers snuggled deep.
I know my dreams are in my head,
But does my head stay in my bed?

Questions like the ones raised in the poem above can lead to further reading, discussion, writing about dreams, and other language arts activities. Poetry can evoke the kind of thoughtfulness that prompts students to ask questions about themselves and their world. Their questions and subsequent search for answers can be the motivating forces for a variety of communication activities that build skills and develop positive attitudes toward engaging in those activities.

Poems That Foster Creative Thinking

A poem can be the springboard to ideas and feelings beyond a student's immediate experiences. It can be the vehicle that enables students to merge their personal experiences with the poet's experience to create new understandings, beliefs, and feelings. Jennings (1965) says, "The one aspect of mature reading that appears most obvious and immediate is the difference we feel within ourselves as a consequence of this reading. This may be as trivial as a matter of having read one more book or as great as a turn-about in political belief or religious conviction" (p. 142).

In more technical terms, creative thinking can be said to occur at the cognitive level of synthesis, defined by Bloom et al. (1965) as "the putting together of elements and parts so as to form a whole. This is a process of working with elements, parts, etc., and combining them in such a way as to constitute a pattern or structure not clearly there before" (p. 162).

Fisher and Terry (1982) comment pertinently:

> As we begin to accept diversity in life-style and values, it becomes more important for students to explore a variety of responses to their environment. In society today there is a wide range of attitudes, opinions, and values; some of these contradict one another. Children must learn to cope with these contradictions and even recognize and communicate their own diversity. They must find what is uniquely personal, what their potential is, and where they stand. Language arts teachers are becoming more interested in imaginative writing—in all areas of written composition—where there is an opportunity for original thought and expression. (p. 180)

Much poetry written for children is well suited for the fostering of creative thinking because it is imaginative and provocative of playful thinking. The rush of an idea or ideas from a poem can encourage students to release their own creative thoughts. For example:

IMAGINING BY THE SEA

I think that I will always like
To walk beside the sea,
Imagining I'm lots of things
That I can never be.

Imagining that I'm a wave
Washing this white beach,
Stretching water fingers out
As far as they will reach.

Imagining that I'm a shark,
The biggest ever seen;
Scaring fishes left and right,
'Cause I'm so hungry-mean.

Imagining that I'm a gull
Resting on a piling, then
Flapping up above the waves,
Fishing while I'm flying.

Imagining that I'm a fish,
A dolphin with a snout,
Sewing up an ocean path
By dipping in and out.

Imagining I'm anything
That's part of this old sea,
Until a sand burr bites my toe.
And then I know I'm me.

Students who live in a city might be asked to imagine they are anything that is part of that city (for example, a subway, a skyscraper, a taxi) and write a stanza or paragraph about their thoughts as that something. Students who live in a rural area might do likewise with silos, wooded trails, pick-up trucks, or other familiar aspects of their environment.

Teachers who stimulate creative thinking are following the advice of Kahil Gibran (1965) who in *The Prophet* wrote that if a teacher "is indeed wise he does not bid you enter the house of his wisdom, but rather leads you to the threshold of your own mind" (p. 56).

Because poems invite and evoke personal additions to the poet's message, they can be the starting points for creative thought. For example, the following tasks might be assigned relative to the reading of a poem: create a different title for this poem, describe the physical appearance of the narrator of this poem, as you imagine it to be, write a note to the poet, add a stanza to this poem, or draw a picture of any stanza in this poem. Tasks that require creative thinking (1) ask for information that is not in the poem itself, (2) cannot be evaluated as correct or incorrect, and (3) focus the student's attention on her or his addition to the poet's creation. Creative thinking tasks are purposefully directed, have parameters, and result in a product students can share with others. Poems lend themselves well to the assignment of language arts activities that result in products that are the result of creative thinking.

Poems That Stimulate Mental Images

Discussions about the phenomenon of mental imagery occasionally turn up people who attest to their inability to get "pictures" in their minds. As a person who conjures up mental images at the drop of a word I am hard pressed to imagine the absence of visual imagery in one's life, but I am prepared to acknowledge that some people either cannot or do not form mental images. I do not think they are many, but I know these people must miss much of the grandeur of the communication arts.

I do know from my teaching experiences that many students need inducement to form mental images as they engage in various forms of communication and thereby to take full advantage of reading, writing, speaking, and listening experiences. Students, for example, who decode the words on a page may get the essence of the author's message, but if they do not take the time to form the mental images suggested by the words, they are likely to find the passage boring and may be able to produce only superficial knowledge of the content. I am convinced that students who form mental images, both as senders and receivers of messages, are higher achievers in school than those who do not. Poetry can be a good medium for teaching students the power of mental imagery for improving reading and listening comprehension as well as for increasing the enjoyment they receive from communication activities. The words from which poems are made sketch images sharply and surely:

WHAT HAPPENED?

What happened to our yard last night?
Come here and look around.
Why, you can see all kinds of things
Lying on the ground.

Sidewalk full of half-drowned worms,
Street all muddy-wet,
Grass all strewn with parts of trees,
Garbage cans upset.

Water's dripping everywhere—
Sliding from green leaves,
Gliding down slick window panes,
Slipping off the eaves.

Trickling down the driveway,
Two streams of water meet,
And search beneath some leaves and twigs
Before they find the street.

I know what's happened to our yard.
It's had a bath, I'll bet.
All the dirt's still in the tub.
And the water's not out yet.

Students might be told before they read or listen to "What Happened?" or some other descriptive poem to get a picture in their minds for each stanza. After reading the poem they might describe their mental pictures

orally or in writing. Dillingofski (1980) reports, "Induced imagery strategies encourage readers to generate appropriate images in their minds as
they read passages. The picture in your mind metaphor succinctly describes
these learner-generated visual images. For example, if the passage describes
the signing of the Declaration of Independence the reader would be
encouraged to visualize the details of the scene" (p. 18). Children's poetry is
rich in visual imagery and is, therefore, fertile ground for imagery training.

Poems for Corrective Readers

Elementary grades teachers always know who corrective readers are when
they are identified as the "kids in your low reading group." They make
progress in their classroom program, but at a slower rate than their
classmates. Their skills weaknesses may be more apparent in reading and
writing, but they usually are slower in listening and speaking skills
development, too. Because learning to read is hard for them, they are
reluctant readers. They are inclined to perceive reading and the other
language arts as series of exercises to be completed in textbooks, kits, and
workbooks instead of as communication processes. That perception has
been taught and perpetuated by the kinds of instructional programs
designed for them. Moffett (1968) says:

> Conventionally . . . poor readers whose problems go beyond decoding
> . . . are made to undergo the sort of dull, mechanical course that actually
> requires the "most" motivation, confidence and maturity to get through.
> They submit to "practice readers," "word study" workbooks, "skill
> builders," "spellers," and so on. Remediation that consists of relentless
> drills and comprehension questions is based on a false assumption that
> the underlying problems are reading problems, whereas the problems are
> ones that "manifest" themselves in reading as elsewhere. For these
> children reading should be more, not less, fun than for others. (p. 112)

Poetry provides an excellent materials supplement or alternative for
underachieving, reluctant users of the language arts.

As was discussed earlier in this chapter, poems with strong rhythm are
excellent for improving the fluency of oral reading. Since a common and
predominant characteristic of corrective readers is expressionless, word-by-
word reading, poems for oral reading practice are especially helpful to their
reading growth. Allington (1983) observes, "Successful beginning readers
receive more encouragement to 'read with expression.' Too often slow first
grade learners receive large doses of letter, sound, and word instruction to
the neglect of larger units of text-like sentences and stories. . . . Good
readers are more likely to get 'meaning-oriented' instruction and to have

their attention focused on 'making sense' or 'sounding right' when reading orally" (p. 558). He adds, "Successful readers are more often reading material that is relatively easy for them, thereby facilitating their translation to fluent reading. Several investigators have reported that poorer readers are more often working with material that is difficult for them. This may inhibit their development of fluent oral reading" (p. 558). Clearly, carefully selected poems can be highly effective material for training corrective readers to read orally with good fluency, a behavior considered by many reading educators to be basic to the development of reading comprehension skills.

Just as rhythm makes many poems especially useful for the needs of corrective readers, so does rhyme. For one thing, rhyme makes the ends of lines more predictable for poor readers, thereby boosting their confidence and their reading fluency. Furthermore, rhyming words can be used very effectively for teaching phonics to poor readers, an aspect of reading that corrective readers find very difficult. Analyzing words that rhyme is a good beginning point for students who find the making of letter-sound relationships difficult.

Riddle poems can be especially instructive for corrective readers. They can be used to teach students to read carefully, searching for clues and thinking ahead as they read. Corrective readers are often careless, superficial readers and need strong motivation to be otherwise. The following exemplifies a poem that can be used very effectively by exposing a stanza at a time and asking students to guess what "it" is on the basis of the accumulation of clues:

The Bravest Thing I Know

It has a long, long way to go,
And it must travel very slow.

Danger lies on every side.
There's no way it can catch a ride.

High above, a hungry hawk!
It cannot run. It still must walk.

On the left, a speeding car!
It can't turn back. It's gone too far.

It has no fear of getting lost,
Inch by inch the road is crossed.

What's the bravest thing I know?
A caterpillar on the go!

The shortness of poems is another commendable feature that recommends them for use with corrective readers. Corrective readers are often defeated a third or less of the way through a reading selection by the fatigue they experience from decoding the language. The skills they possess become increasingly weaker as they plod through a story. When they read the end of the story, they often feel more frustration than satisfaction, because of their fatigue. In addition, their comprehension is minimal causing them to feel cheated as they stumble through the final paragraph. Short poems give corrective readers the opportunity to read the whole piece with understanding and pleasure before their skills are overtaxed.

Finally, the ease of conjuring up mental images with poetry is another characteristic that makes it especially appealing for use with corrective readers. These students are so intent upon just reading the words right that they do not image unless the stimulus is strong. Carefully selected poems can provide the strong stimulation that is needed to produce images that enhance comprehension and appreciation.

All in all, the characteristics of poems that make them advantageous for the attainment of reading and language arts curriculum objectives for average and above average students make them even more so for underachievers. I strongly recommend their use with students at all ability levels.

SUMMARY

In summary, teachers must not overlook the potential of children's poetry for the attainment of the cognitive as well as the affective goals of reading and language arts curricula. Many poems have characteristics (rhythm, rhyme, shortness) that make them more valuable for the development of language arts skills than materials typically used for that purpose. Furthermore, these characteristics make poetry especially helpful in the reading, writing, speaking, and listening skills development of underachievers. Carefully selected poems can help students at all ability levels learn how their language works and how to work their language. The key lies in the willingness of teachers to use poems for more than the development of appreciation and in their skillfulness in using them to teach specific language arts skills.

REFERENCES

Allington, Richard L. "Fluency: The Neglected Reading Goal." *The Reading Teacher* 366 (February 1983): 556–61.

Bates, Gary W. "The Comparative Effects of Two Mathemagenic Activities in Ninth-Grade Good and Poor Readers' Comprehension, Retention, and Attitudes." Ph.D. dissertation, University of Wisconsin–Madison, 1981.

Bloom, Benjamin S.; Engelhart, Max D.; Furst, Edward J.; Hill, Walker H.; & Krathwohl, David R. *Taxonomy of Educational Objectives.* New York: David McKay, 1965.

Burns, Paul C. & Broman, Betty L. *The Language Arts in Childhood Education.* 5th ed. Boston: Houghton Mifflin, 1983.

Dillingofski, Mary Sue. "The Effects of Imposed and Induced Visual Imagery Strategies on Ninth Grade Difference-Poor Readers' Literal Comprehension of Concrete and Abstract Prose." Ph.D. dissertation, University of Wisconsin–Madison, 1980.

Fisher, Carol J. & Terry, Ann C. *Children's Language and the Language Arts.* New York: McGraw-Hill, 1982.

Gibran, Kahlil. *The Prophet.* New York: Knopf, 1965.

Jennings, Frank. *This Is Reading.* New York: Bureau of Publications, Teachers College, Columbia University, 1965.

Kean, John M. & Personke, Carl. *The Language Arts: Teaching and Learning in the Elementary Schools.* New York: St. Martin's, 1976.

Moffett, James. *A Student-Centered Language Arts Curriculum, Grades K–6: A Handbook for Teachers.* Boston: Houghton Mifflin, 1968.

Pilon, Barbara A. *Teaching Language Arts Creatively in the Elementary Grades.* New York: John Wiley and Sons, 1978.

Smith, Frank. *Understanding Reading: A Psycholinguistic Analysis of Reading and Learning to Read.* 2nd ed. New York: Holt, Rinehart & Winston, 1978.

Stewig, John Warren. *Children and Literature.* Chicago: Rand McNally College Publication Co., 1980.

Wolsch, Robert A. & Wolsch, Lois A. *From Speaking to Writing to Reading: Relating the Arts of Communication.* New York: Teachers College Press, 1982.

CHAPTER 2

Children's Poetry Preferences

The continuing availability of children's poetry books in bookstores and supermarkets is good evidence that children's poetry has not lost its market appeal. Most children have books bought for them, and many of those books contain poems. Adults like to read poems to children, and children learn to enjoy the rhythms and sounds of poetry. A developmental milestone in many families is a child's first recitation of Humpty Dumpty or some other nursery rhyme.

The delight most preschool children derive from poetry should be nurtured and heightened by appropriate schoolwork. One of the major instructional objectives of teachers should be to maintain the positive attitudes toward poetry most children have when they enter kindergarten or first grade and begin their formal instruction in the English language arts. Using poetry for skills instruction as well as literary appreciation need not interfere with that objective.

Children's attitudes toward poetry are formed by their experiences. I am reminded of a class of first graders whose teacher frequently played a phonograph of children's poems, read to the accompaniment of a guitar. The children loved the record and asked to hear it long after they knew the poems by heart. Something about the poems and how they were presented caused the children never to say, "Do we have to listen to that record again?" Certainly the teacher, the classroom, the guitar music, and other factors influenced the children's attitudes toward that record as they listened to it again and again. However, much credit has to be given to the poems themselves. Children do have poetry preferences, and teachers should be aware of those preferences when they choose poems for their students. Stewig (1980, p. 232) says:

> Teachers and librarians must examine the kinds of poems being shared with children and the nature of that experience. They should consider these questions when choosing poetry to share:
>
> 1. "Is the poem something I can read effectively?" Even if a poem is topical or by a famous poet, a teacher must make sure he or she likes it. A reader must like a poem to read it well.

16

2. "Is the poem different in form or content from other things I've shared recently?" All teachers have preferences, however unexamined. They need to look analytically at what they choose to make sure they present a wide variety of ideas and styles.
3. "Will the poem appeal to both boys and girls?" Children, both boys and girls, are interested in verses that present a clear and unusual view, poems in which something active happens, or humorous poems.

Two studies provide more specific guidance in regard to the selection of poetry for children based on the children's preferences. One (Terry, 1974) investigated the poetry preferences of children in grades four, five, and six. The other (Fisher & Natarella, 1982) investigated the poetry preferences of children in grades one, two, and three from the same schools that Terry used in her study. The findings of these two studies are critical for teachers who teach poetry for the purpose of developing language arts skills as well as for appreciation. Fisher and Natarella point out, "A consistent finding in studies of children's preferences for poetry is that adults cannot accurately predict which poems children will like; their choices of poems for children seldom match the children's own choices" (p. 339).

For her study of children's poetry preferences, Terry sampled 422 fourth, fifth, and sixth graders, drawn at random from forty-five schools. The schools were randomly selected from the states of Florida, Ohio, Pennsylvania, and Texas, which had been randomly selected from four geographic regions of the country.

One hundred thirteen poems were tested with the children. The poems were suggested by two professors of children's literature, two upper elementary grades teachers, and an earlier researcher into children's poetry preferences. They were asked to consider form, content, poetic elements, and age of the poems when they made their suggestions. The poems were recorded on cassette tapes by a radio announcer, who was experienced with reading poetry.

The children listened to ten to twelve poems a day over a period of ten days. The children heard each poem twice before responding to the following three questions, which were graded on a five-point scale: (1) How much do you like this poem? (2) Would you like to hear this poem again? (3) Could this be one of your favorite poems? In addition, the children's teachers were surveyed to discover their own poetry preferences and their use of it in the classroom.

The key findings of the Terry study were as follows:

1. Children's enthusiasm for poetry declines as they advance from fourth to sixth grade.

2. In poetry, children in grades four through six respond most favorably to contemporary, rather than traditional poems; poems about familiar, enjoyable experiences; poems that tell stories; poems that have a strong element of humor; poems with rhythm and rhyme; and poems that do not rely heavily on complex imagery or subtle implications.
3. The majority of teachers pay little attention to poetry in class and seldom read it to their students or encourage them to write their own poems.

For their study of first, second, and third graders' preferences, Fisher and Natarella categorized sixty-four poems according to four factors. One factor was form; narrative poems, free verse, rhymed verse, lyric poetry, limericks, and haiku were selected for that category. Another factor was topic; poems about nature, animals, children, childhood experiences, and the strange and fantastic were included. A third factor was the presence of certain poetic elements such as rhyme, metaphorical language, and onomatopoeia. Fourthly, poems were chosen to represent traditional and modern poems. Traditional poetry was defined as poetry written forty or more years ago and found in most anthologies of poetry for young children. The modern poems were recent publications and were about various aspects of modern life such as telephones, cars, H-bombs, and junkyards.

The students in the Fisher and Natarella study listened to eight poems a day for eight days and scored each poem. They were instructed to give each poem they really liked a star, each poem they thought was all right an OK, and each poem they did not like a No. The star and the OK responses were given points of three and two, respectively. The No responses received one point. In addition, the children's teachers were asked to write down the children's comments about why they liked or disliked the various poems.

Overall, the poems received high scores, showing that the children liked listening to the poems. However, statistical analyses of the scores the children gave the poems revealed some definite and strong preferences. The poetic element for which the children showed their strongest preference was rhyme. They also preferred poems with rhythm, poems that were funny, poems about animals, and poems about familiar experiences. They disliked free verse and haiku. They also disliked the use of imagery and figurative language.

Taken together, the studies show that children in grades one through six have surprisingly similar poetry preferences.

The poems that appear in chapters four and five of this book were written in accordance with the major findings of the two studies described above. They are about enjoyable experiences, familiar to today's child; they tell a story; they contain an element of humor; they rhyme, and they have clearly identifiable rhythms. They were also written with an eye to their being used for specific skills development. Therefore, elementary grades teachers should find them suitable for students' affective and cognitive development.

Libraries and bookstores are other sources of poems for elementary grades teachers to use with their students for the development of specific reading and language arts skills as well as for the development of literary appreciation. The following annotated bibliography was prepared by two reading specialists (Velma Dauer, Edgerton, Wisconsin Public Schools; Dale Wortley, Madison, Wisconsin Metropolitan School District) who have had considerable experience using poetry according to the philosophy and guidelines presented in this book. The books they include in their bibliography are available in most libraries that have collections of children's poetry and in bookstores.

POETRY FOR USE IN ELEMENTARY CLASSROOMS:
AN ANNOTATED BIBLIOGRAPHY

Bennett, Jill (Ed.). *Roger Was A Razor Fish*. Illustrated by Maureen Roffey. New York: Lothrop, Lee, and Shepard Books, 1980.

Twenty-two short, rhyming verses by such poets as Myra Cohn Livingston, Aileen Fisher, Rose Fyleman, and Robert Frost offer an easy-to-read experience in poetry for the beginning or less advanced reader. The text format and illustrations are attractive and inviting.

The interesting, descriptive language found in the poem "Buildings" by Myra Cohn Livingston could be a model from which students could conjure up their own experiential knowledge about the topic. Their ideas and mental images could be translated into a mural illustrating a variety of buildings on a street. For vocabulary development each building could be labeled. A discussion of each building's uniqueness would help develop language and discrimination skills.

John Ciardi's "What Someone Said When He Was Spanked on the Day Before His Birthday" presents in a humorous way a young child's thoughts about running away from home. The cumulative and sequential verses lend themselves well to predicting and inferential thinking. Stanzas could be presented one-by-one for discussion of such questions as: Have you ever felt like running away? Why? What happened? What are some reasons why people run away? What do you think caused the main character in this poem to want to run away? Why do you suppose the main character decided to stay and not run away? Where would you run away to?

"Roger Was a Razor Fish" by Al Pittman could lead students to make a list of different kinds of fish. Each fish could be given an alliterative name and illustrated. The Dr. Seuss book *One Fish, Two Fish* could be read to extend this reading experience.

The reader or listener could infer what things probably make the child in Aileen Fisher's "My Puppy" happy and grumpy. This poem could also be useful for inductively teaching the short *u* sound. Students might enjoy dictating and reading a language experience story using "My Puppy" as a stimulus.

> Blishen, Edward (Ed.). *The Oxford Book of Poetry for Children.* Illustrated by Brian Wildsmith. New York: Oxford University Press, 1982.

Blishen has compiled a poetry anthology to "help children make the leap from nursery rhyme to 'serious' verse." He has thematically arranged 150 pages of poems from English literature that offer a nice balance to other more contemporary collections. The reader will find poems of humor, mystery, nature, and people as well as limericks. The award-winning illustrations are charming and colorful. There is something for everyone in this book of poems, which is meant to be shared by the child and the adult. Many of the poems are short enough in length, rhyming in structure, and interesting enough in content to lend themselves well for the purpose of reading instruction for reluctant readers.

"AEIOU" by Jonathan Swift is an eight-line poem offering a richness of reading activities. It can become a thinking riddle by omitting the title. Young readers could be asked to use context clues to identify the main idea or what they think the title might be. Students could construct lists of words with the same vowel sounds as those highlighted in the poem. Additionally, this poem lends itself well to small group choral reading.

William Allington's "Four Ducks on a Pond" is another short treasure for that "feeling" part of us all. It offers a simple, but rich, model for writing poetry about those special, individual things in our daily lives that are most meaningful to us. The language is excellent for inducing images that students could then illustrate.

"The Snail" by James Reeves lends itself well to being presented to students as a cloze exercise. By using context clues, students can predict deleted rhyming words. This can either be done as a group, using an overhead transparency, or individually on a reproduced work sheet. The language, while clear and compact, is rich and requires careful thinking. Students' vocabularies could be expanded through discussion of multiple-meaning words such as *bank*.

Imaginations and mental imagery can flourish while reading or listening to "The Magnifying Glass" by Walter de la Mare. The title could be omitted so that students could use context clues to determine the subject. Students could discuss how their experiential backgrounds helped them determine the subject. Details of what the author saw with his "magnifying glass" could be recalled and creatively illustrated. Students could even imagine and illustrate an idea of their own under the "magnifying glass." Vocabulary words such as *myriad* provide skill practice in learning meaning from context.

There is a poem to interest just about every student in this book. A reading group could select, practice reading, and present a carnival of poems using background music, tape recorders, costumes, overhead projectors, and the like.

Calmenson, Stephan (Ed.). *Never Take a Pig to Lunch and Other Funny Poems About Animals.* Illustrations by Hilary Knight. Garden City, N.Y.: Doubleday, 1982.

As the title promises, this is a collection of funny poems about animals. Most of the twenty-five poems are short and contain vocabulary suitable for beginning readers. Several of the poems could be used to teach or practice word identification skills. For example, "I Wouldn't," which describes a cat asking the mice to come out to play, could be used to focus on spelling patterns of ___ay, or ___at. "Hippopotamus" by Rachel Phillips works well to review short *i* words. (By the way, when we teach word identification skills with poetry, we read and enjoy the poem at the beginning of the lesson; at the end of the lesson we do the same—that way the skill is practiced in the context of whole language.) For the dog lovers in the classroom, Jack Kent's "Puppies" should be a winner! This poem, which lends itself to oral reading, describes a home in which puppies populate practically every corner of the house. Students from a small group could be assigned lines, rehearse their parts individually, then put it all together for a class presentation.

Ciardi, John. *You Read to Me, I'll Read to You.* Drawings by Edward Gorey. New York: Lippincott, 1962.

"All the poems printed in black, you read to me. All the poems printed in blue, I'll read to you." This is the directive for this collection of thirty-five humorous poems with engaging illustrations.

"About Jimmy James" has a couplet rhyming pattern. The stanzas tell a cumulative story that can then be sequenced. After reading or listening to the poem, students could retell the sequence of events orally, through a series of illustrations or by cutting and pasting scrambled verses. Individual or small groups of students could present a choral reading of the poem to other students. This poem can also be used to encourage inferential thinking and responding to such questions as: Why do you suppose Jimmy James was so intent on running away? How do you think his family felt about his desire to run away? What makes you come to that conclusion? Why do you think they probably felt this way? What do you think happened to Jimmy James in the end? Which key words support your view?

Before reading "The Wise Hen" the teacher could have students predict the story from the title. After some predictions are made the teacher might read the first stanza of the poem, then pause to let the students make new predictions based on the clues in the first verse. Questions related to the fox/hen relationship could be discussed to enhance comprehension of the text. Students might then make inferences about why the hen said she liked to be dry, but decided in the end to get wet.

"One Day" is an amusing, three-stanza poem requiring a lot of mental imagery. After becoming familiar with the poem, students could illustrate, on a three-sectioned accordion strip of paper, their mental images in sequential order. The vocabulary in this poem can be used to teach or reinforce the short *i* sound and the vowel variants *ou* and *ow*.

The last poem in this book is interestingly untitled and in rhyming couplet form. The skill of identifying the main idea can be taught by reading the poem to the students, without letting them see the illustrations. The children could then be asked to write a title for the poem based on what they think the main idea or central thought of the poem is. Their titles could be shared and their reasons for creating the titles discussed. Rhyming banks, like word banks, could be developed to be used as a resource for student poetry writing. The teacher could list each key rhyming word from the poem on a work sheet and students could write down as many words as they can that rhyme with the key word.

Cole, William (Ed.). *Poem Stew*. Illustrated by Karen Ann Weinhaus. New York: Lippincott, 1981.

Can you imagine cooking up a batch of "Rhinoceros Stew"? The recipe is contained in a poem by Mildred Luton. This collection is filled with outrageous and preposterous poems, reflecting humorously on the topic of food in one way or another. Many are one to four stanzas in length, a nice length for a variety of reading and language arts objectives. William Cole's "A Cucumber's Pickle" offers opportunities for vocabulary development with such interesting words as *contemplate* and *oblivious*. Students could predict the meaning of these words from context clues and check the accuracy of their predictions with a dictionary. Using "Lasagna," a four-line poem by X. J. Kennedy, as a pattern, students could exercise their creative thinking by developing their own one-stanza poem. "The Silver Fish" by Shel Silverstein requires the reader to draw inferences and can be used to help students understand that they must draw upon both their own experiences and what the poet has stated in order to understand the poem.

   Cole, William (Ed.). *Dinosaurs and Beasts of Yore*. Cleveland: Collins, 1979.

Dinosaur lovers will enjoy this collection of short, humorous poems about dinosaurs and other now-extinct creatures. Many poems are two to four lines in length, while a few are one page long. While some require background knowledge that young children may not have (for example, the poem that draws the analogy between dinosaurs and the Edsel), many are suitable for elementary students. We have found that second graders in particular love dinosaurs and find these poems delightful.

   The visual images evoked in "Take My Advice" (what to do if you ever meet a diplodocus) or "Dudley Not Cuddly" (why the wooly mammoth pet had to be let go) could be illustrated on filmstrip material. Children could then practice and tape record the poems that accompany their illustrations. Seven or eight of these illustration/poetry combinations would make a nice presentation for the whole class or another classroom, while at the same time accomplishing oral reading and comprehension objectives. A little music fading in and out between poetry readers on the tape adds a professional touch.

   Cole, William (Ed.). *Oh, Such Foolishness*. Pictures by Tomie de Paola. New York: Lippincott, 1978.

The whimsical and zany verses and drawings in this book are the kind that are preferred by children. Students can predict deleted rhyming words for a clozure exercise using "An Alphabet of Questions" by Charles Edward Carryl. These amusing, alliterative questions about animals can also reinforce beginning sound/symbol knowledge. Children can pattern their own "Alphabet of Questions" transforming the category of animals into alliterative questions about the categories of food, toys, clothing, countries, and so on.

   "Foolish Questions" by William Cole offers the reader or listener the pleasure of playing with the multiple meanings of words. Vocabulary words from the poem can be used to write and illustrate sentences with homonyms. A link with children's literature can be extended by reading

Amelia Bedilia by Peggy Parrish and *The King Who Rained* by Fred Gwynne. Making humorous homonym books patterned after *The King Who Rained* is a favorite activity of students.

Lines could gradually be uncovered and context clues used for the skill of prediction while reading "If Things Grew Down" by Robert D. Hoeft. "A cat would grow (into a kitten), your sweater would grow (into a mitten)." The variant vowel combination of *ow* could be taught or reviewed. Students could create additional couplets for the poem. The teacher might read books of other unusual reversed situations such as *The Shrinking of Treehorn* by Florence Parry Heide and *Cloudy with a Chance of Meatballs* by Judi Barrett.

> Golden Book. *A Child's First Book of Poems*. Pictures by Cyndy Szekeres. Racine, Wis.: Western Publishing Co., 1981.

This beautifully illustrated collection of thirty-six poems was compiled especially for the young listener or reader. Most of the poems are short, and many lend themselves to activities related to comprehension, word identification, or oral reading, as well as language experience follow-up activities. Fifteen of the poems are about animals. After reading or listening to "Cats" by Eleanor Farjeon, students could recall the details from the poem and produce a mural to illustrate the various places one might encounter a cat sleeping. Rose Fyleman's "Mice" is a good example of descriptive writing and could provide a pattern for children's own writing. "Like a Bug" by Aileen Fisher asks the reader or listener to consider what it would be like to be a bug; we have found this poem useful for teaching the —*ug* spelling pattern.

Many of the poems are about childhood experiences. One of these is "New Shoes" by Marjorie Seymour Watts, which could serve as a review for two spellings of the long *e* sound. "Clouds" by Christina Rossetti, a favorite of one of the reviewer's first grade Navajo students of some years ago, is a good poem for language experience follow-up activities, such as illustrating cloud shapes and writing about them. "Hiding" by Dorothy Aldis is especially good for oral reading, since it is a longer poem (eight stanzas) and contains some dialogue. It could be used either with individual students or as a choral reading—in either case, young readers would enjoy and benefit from rehearsing their parts.

> Larrick, Nancy (Ed.). *Piping down the Valleys Wild*. Illustrated by Ellen Raskin. New York: Dell, 1968.

In her introduction, Larrick remarks that she has found children "particularly responsive to the simple, almost conversational language of modern verse. They prefer poems that are fresh and crisp to those they consider 'too sweet'" (p. xxii). According to Larrick, the poems in this collection were read to or read by children and were preferred by them over hundreds of other poems.

A collection of over 200 poems, this book is divided into several sections, including "Sing a song of laughter . . ." (humorous poetry); "I saw a spooky witch out riding on her broom" (spooky poems); "I'd take the hound with the drooping ear . . ." (poems about animals); and more. It is a collection that has appeal for all ages.

Of particular value for reading and language arts instruction are the humorous poems. For example, "Mummy Slept Late and Daddy Fixed Breakfast" by John Ciardi relates to the experience of a child whose father is not particularly good at cooking—breakfast, at least. This poem works well as a cloze exercise to help students use context clues to make "educated guesses" about what words make sense for deleted words in the poem. If you have never prepared material for cloze activities before, here are a few hints: Delete only one or possibly two words in each stanza and replace each with a blank; this will allow students to have enough language to serve as clues in order to make good guesses for the deleted words. Have students read the entire poem silently, then attempt to fill in the cloze blanks. Also, be sure to discuss students' suggestions for the words that have been deleted and compare them to the original. (The overhead projector may be used, or students may each have a copy of the poem.)

Several limericks and short poems can be found in the humorous section. Students from a reading group could rehearse favorite limericks and short poems, read them into a tape recorder (with a little musical background between performers), and present this "program" to the whole class.

MacLeod, Doug. *In the Garden of Badthings*. Pictures by Peter Thomson. New York: Puffin Books, Penguin, 1982.

Children love the bizarre, grotesque, scary poems and illustrations in this small book, which houses twenty short and rhyming verses.

"In the Garden of Badthings" can be used to teach the use of context clues for predicting rhyming words. The meanings of some vocabulary words such as *nestle* and *domain* can also be learned by using context clues. The poem is also useful for expressive oral reading and mental imagery training.

Teachers could delete rhyming words from "Vampire Visit" for instruction in using context clues. The verses tell a sequentially organized story. Students could use context clues to unscramble the scrambled verses and arrange them in the correct order. The poem is also good for choral reading.

For instruction related to the letter *o*, the poem "O's" is just what the teacher ordered. The thirty-three *o* words from the poem representing the long and short sounds of *o* could be categorized into two groups. Students could also supply and categorize words with the long and short sounds of other vowels.

> Prelutsky, Jack (Ed.). *The Random House Book of Poetry for Children.* Illustrated by Arnold Lobel. New York: Random House, 1983.

Prelutsky states in his introduction to this collection of 572 poems, "I tried to fill this book with poems I believe elementary school children will like" (p. 19). He used as selection criteria the characteristics of rhythm, rhyme, imagery, and appeal to children's interests. Absent from this collection are long narrative poems frequently found in other anthologies because Prelutsky felt these would not be of interest to today's children. Instead, he has placed the focus of this collection on humor and light verse.

Simply flipping the pages will reveal dozens of short poems useful for reading and language arts activities. Since the book is thematically organized, it is easy to locate poems on specific topics. To help the user locate favorite titles, there are three indexes: title, first lines, and author. A subject index is also included.

To make good use of this collection in the reading and language arts programs, one could skim through the various sections (probably beginning with "Dogs and Cats and Bears and Bats" and proceeding to "Children, Children Everywhere" and "Nonsense! Nonsense!") to identify and list poems suitable for various objectives, such as the following: working with context clues through cloze exercises, vocabulary development, predicting, imaging, word identification skills, expressive oral reading, or follow-up language experience activities. Such a list of poems and objectives developed especially for the particular reading groups or class with which one is working is useful for lesson planning and helps insure that many different types of activities are incorporated into instructional plans.

For instance, the five-stanza poem titled "The Camel's Complaint" by Charles E. Carryl works well as a choral reading because it has a repetitious line at the end of each stanza. "Cat's Menu" by Richard Shaw could provide the stimulus for a follow-up activity of writing a menu for a pet, using all sorts of interesting, descriptive words. "Eat-it-all Elaine" describes a girl at summer camp who eats whatever inedible item is handy at the time. "Eat-it-all Elaine" would work well to teach the use of context clues, since its length and theme provide enough language and ideas to make it quite predictable. The four-line poem "Josephine" by Alexander Resnikoff could serve as a pattern for children to develop their own nonsense poetry in this way: instead of "Josephine, Josephine, The meanest girl I've ever seen," students could substitute another three-syllable name and change *meanest* to another adjective; then following the pattern of Resnikoff's last two lines of "Her eyes are red, her hair is green, and she takes baths in gasoline," students could complete the last two lines with a description of the person and what she or he is noted for doing.

Prelutsky, Jack. *Zoo Doings.* Illustrated by Paul O. Zelinsky. New York: Greenwillow Books, 1983.

The focus of this book of short poems is on animals, as one might guess by the title. Included are poems that offer warnings such as "Don't Ever Seize a Weasel by the Tail" and "The Bengal Tiger," which tells the reader or listener how to prevent becoming hypnotized by this big cat. Other poems are descriptive or are commentaries on the way of life of the animal, such as "The Beaver," "The Lion," and "The Ostrich."

After reading and enjoying a few of these poems to get a "feeling" for the style, students might predict ideas other poems will contain, basing their predictions on the poem titles. These predictions can be written on the chalkboard and compared to the poems after reading them. Following this activity, it is good to get more "mileage" out of the poems by helping students to read them orally with good expression.

Prelutsky, Jack. *The Baby Uggs Are Hatching.* Illustrations by James Stevenson. New York: Greenwillow Books, 1982.

Out of Prelutsky's wild and creative imagination has emerged this set of twelve poems about strange, imaginary creatures—most of which gobble up whatever is in sight, or are capable of doing so. Many of the poems have the potential for helping students expand their vocabulary. "The Quossible," a four-stanza poem, is one example. Fourth graders with whom we have used this poem enjoyed predicting the meanings of words like *irascible* and *deplorable*, then confirming (or modifying) their predictions with a dictionary. This activity works well with teams of two students. (By the way, it is important to have a good standard dictionary handy for some of the interesting vocabulary found in Prelutsky's poems—many words cannot be found in a typical intermediate dictionary.) "The Smasheroo," a poem about a monster who loves to smash things to bits, contains more interesting words: *devastated, disintegrated, decimated.*

To provide practice in using clues from the poem to visualize Prelutsky's creatures, this activity could be used as follows: (1) present a poem without the illustration; (2) assign a small group of students to work together to make a large drawing of the creature described in the poem, based on clues provided by the poet; and (3) have students compare their representation of the creature to that of the illustrator, James Stevenson.

Prelutsky, Jack. *Kermit's Garden of Verses.* Illustrated by Bruce McNally. New York: Random House, 1982.

The favorite characters from Muppetland are found in this compact book of thirty short, rhyming verses. The prior knowledge that most young readers have about the Muppets facilitates motivation and comprehension. Students can recall some of the things that make Kermit happy after they have read or listened to "When the Temperature Is Rising." They can also use context clues to predict rhyming words as well as discuss and share the mental images that the language in this poem induces.

"Miss Piggy" provides an opportunity to practice the skill of recalling facts, along with teaching or reinforcing the concepts of antonyms such as *sad* and *glad* and the long and short vowel sounds for the letter *a*. The verses of this poem provide good material for choral reading. An extended writing activity can be to have children write rhyming couplets about

"_____makes me feel glad,
But _____makes me sad."

Context clues can be used to predict deleted rhyming words in the poem "My Garden." Students could also use context clues to discover the meaning of such vocabulary words as *putter, cultivate, frantic,* and *calm.* They could then confirm or reject their meanings by checking with the dictionary. This poem also lends itself to a discussion about where individuals go to "escape." Visual images of Kermit's garden, or individual "escape" places, offer many possibilities for sharing and illustrating personal experiences.

Silverstein, Shel. *A Light in the Attic.* Drawings by Shel Silverstein. New York: Harper & Row, 1981.

For a delightful instructional lesson about suffixes, "Ations" cannot be beat. Words in the poem such as *salutation, consideration, altercation,* and *reconciliation* offer the opportunity for vocabulary development. Definitions accompany them, and students could demonstrate understanding of their meaning by creating sentences for each one. A list of additional *-ation* words could be developed, defined, and used in sentences. This poem is also well suited to choral reading.

"Eight Balloons" is especially well structured for recalling facts and sequencing events. It also presents the reader or listener with some delightful mental images of eight balloons on the loose. A group of eight readers could present this poem orally, enlivened by props or illustrations, to the rest of the class.

"Never" is a poem to induce discussion and writing activities about things students have never done, but would like to do someday. Many unusual words, like *lop-eared, swayback,* and *brine,* require young readers to use context clues to predict their meanings.

> Silverstein, Shel. *Where the Sidewalk Ends.* Drawings by Shel Silverstein. New York: Harper & Row, 1974.

These tightly organized, rhyming poems suggest a myriad of reading and language arts instructional activities.

"Captain Hook" can be read to practice the skill of recalling facts. Students can listen to "Jimmy Jet and His TV Set" for mental imagery and the recalling of details. After reading the poem aloud, children could draw what they visualize Jimmy Jet looked like at the end of the poem. Student drawings could be compared with the author's to check the details they remembered to include and the details they forgot.

In "Invention" Silverstein tells about a light that plugs into the sun—a wonderful, energy-saving invention. "But, oh, there's only one thing wrong . . ." At this point in the poem the teacher stops reading aloud and asks students to offer their conclusions about what is wrong with this wonderful invention.

Children love to listen to and predict the rhyming word for each couplet in "Sarah Cynthia Sylvia Stout Would Not Take the Garbage Out." There are enough lines for an entire class to develop a choral reading presentation that could be accompanied by student-made illustrated slides. The most reluctant reader enjoys reading this poem.

A very concrete lesson can be acted out to the poem "Smart." The skill of recalling sequential order is reinforced through the dramatization of what the young child in this poem does with a one dollar bill his father has given him.

One of the more thoughtful poems in this collection is "The Search." After reading or listening to this poem, students can share and discuss some of their personal goals and values in life. A verse could be added to the poem to answer the question posed in the final line, "What do I search for now?" This extended writing activity could be done either as a group or individually.

REFERENCES

Fisher, Carol J. & Natarella, Margaret A. "Young Children's Preferences in Poetry: A National Survey of First, Second, and Third Graders." *Research in the Teaching of English* 16, no. 4 (December 1982): 339-55.

Stewig, John Warren. *Children and Literature*. Chicago: Rand McNally College
    Publishing Co., 1980.
Terry, Ann. *Children's Poetry Preferences: A National Survey of Upper Elementary
    Grades*. Urbana, Ill.: National Council of Teachers of English, 1974.

CHAPTER 3

Poetry in the Reading
and Language Arts Curricula

The primary purpose of reading and language arts instruction is to help people communicate with one another. The word *communicate* comes from the Latin word *communis*, meaning "common." When people communicate, they are establishing a "commonness" with others. Schramm (1973) describes the communication process as follows:

> Communication always requires at least three elements—the source, the message, and the destination. A "source" may be an individual (speaking, writing, drawing, gesturing) or a communication organization (like a newspaper, publishing house, television station, or motion picture studio). The "message" may be in the form of ink on paper, sound waves in the air, impulses in an electric current, a wave of the hand, a flag in the air, or any other signal capable of being interpreted meaningfully. The "destination" may be an individual listening, watching, or reading, or a member of a group, such as a discussion group, a lecture audience, a football crowd or a mob; or an individual member of the particular group we call the "mass audience," such as the reader of a newspaper or a viewer of television. (p. 28)

At the heart of Schramm's description is an important concept, one teachers and students should keep in mind as reading and language arts instruction takes place: communication is a process of sending messages. Speaking and writing require message-sending skills; listening and reading require message-receiving skills. Central to the process is the message. Teachers and students who keep the sender–message–receiver paradigm in mind in the course of instruction are more likely to attain the primary reading and language arts curriculum goals than those who do not. People read, write, speak, and listen to be in personal contact with other people. Teachers who do not keep this purpose in the forefront of their own awareness are likely not to get this idea across to children, and children who do not engage in reading, writing, speaking, and listening activities with this purpose in mind are likely to learn communication

31

skills in a mechanical sense only, or not learn them at all. A mechanically correct message that says nothing meaningful to a reader or listener is wasteful of both the sender's and the receiver's energies.

De Haven (1983) says, "Teaching the language arts is a process that involves helping children develop their knowledge, appreciation, and skillful use of language. Teaching thus requires a master plan to stimulate language awareness and provide opportunities for children to use language purposefully. Language learning is an active process, one that depends upon cognitive responses to stimuli" (p. 460).

The selection of messages for teaching communication skills is one of teachers' most important responsibilities. An interesting phenomenon in the development of children's instructional reading materials has been the shift in concern from the quality of the material to the quantity of skill-development exercises. Some developmental reading materials do contain good quality literature, but it is not difficult to find uninteresting and vacuous writing in materials (especially kits and workbooks) designed for children's instructional reading programs.

It is not surprising that so many children proceed mechanically through their instructional materials with not one thought to impede the completion of the exercises recommended in the teacher's manual. The materials are often uninteresting and content-weak. Smith and Johnson (1980) comment appropriately that

> in too many classrooms, the teaching of reading has deteriorated to the point that teachers have become dispensers of commercial reading materials consisting of short selections with coordinated "things to do" or "questions to answer," prescribed by someone other than the teacher. Dealing in a personal and relaxed atmosphere with ideas and feelings that an author wanted to share with a reader has become a scarce item in too many classrooms. It is not difficult to understand from observations of reading classes why students learn to value a score of 80 percent more than a relationship with Tom Sawyer via the pen of Mark Twain. They have been taught how to answer questions at the expense of being taught how to read. (p. 6)

Bill Martin, Jr. (1967) sums up the situation remarkably well:

> Children come to first grade with the expectation that they can learn to read immediately. They have absorbed this vision of school from their culture. Imagine their disappointment when their early and impressionable reading experiences begin, not in storybooks filled with memorable language, but in tool books that rob language of its wholeness and reduce dreams to boredom. It is my opinion that many, many children never recover from this disappointment. (p. 57).

Language arts curricula have developed somewhat differently. Their goal often appears to be more content oriented, and more attention is given to providing students with good quality messages. Students are asked to appreciate and perhaps analyze the structure and content of speeches, short stories, essays, and poems, but the skills necessary to accomplish these goals are too frequently taught superficially or not at all. Literary selections are presented as if children know how to read them or listen to them; content and appreciation questions are asked as if children know how to find the answers; writing or speaking activities are assigned as if children have already mastered the skills necessary to complete them. Since they do not and have not, the result is lack of understanding and appreciation.

The postures of both the reading curriculum and the language arts curriculum often do not reflect the reality of language skills development. Thinking is at the heart of all reading, writing, speaking, and listening behavior. To develop skills, children's thinking must be applied to meaningful messages, whether those messages are being sent or received. Donoghue (1971) points out that "language is not learned independent of meaning or function. Children do not learn anything about language from anyone (including authors) unless there is a shared sense of purpose and a shared understanding of meaning. If teachers try to present language as a subject consisting of abstract rules and information, the language skills of children will be virtually unaffected" (p. 3). Furthermore, children, at least many children, do not learn reading, writing, speaking, and listening skills simply by "using language." Certainly frequent and varied experiences using language are essential to the development of communication skills, but so is direct and focused instruction that teaches children behaviors that enable them to send and receive messages effectively. Thought-provoking, interesting messages and thought-guiding instruction should be central to reading and language arts instruction in the elementary school. Of course, the instructional power is increased when the messages are also aesthetically appealing and entertaining.

As was pointed out in chapter one, carefully selected poetry has the potential for building reading, writing, speaking, and listening skills as well as being entertaining and aesthetically appealing. It rightfully belongs among the varieties of messages selected for use in reading and language arts curricula.

WHERE DOES POETRY FIT?

Reading and language arts curricula have a basic strand and a supplementary strand. Poetry has a place in both. The basic strand makes up the heart of the program, the systematic, sequential instructional process through which students attain increasing levels of maturity as language users from kindergarten through grade twelve. The supplementary strand reinforces the basic strand. Students' work with supplementary materials and activities helps them to master skills and gain fuller understandings and appreciations. In effect, the supplementary strand provides the extra practice and the more complete insights into language functions that children need to become proficient communicators. The basic strand is the first and the most systematic application; the supplementary strand follows. Both are necessary for a complete curriculum.

This is not a methods textbook, so a thorough discussion of poetry in the reading and language arts curricula is not included. Suffice it to say that poetry has traditionally been taught for its content and form at all grade levels as part of the basic curriculum. It has also been used for specific skills development, but only rarely and then incidentally to other objectives. Its use for supplementary instruction, especially skills instruction, has been rare indeed. Stories and expository discourse have always upstaged it.

From my informal classroom experiments with poetry during the last five years, I have come to two conclusions: (1) poetry can and should be used more than it is for other than aesthetic purposes in the basic strand of the reading and language arts curricula, and (2) it is an excellent vehicle in the supplementary program for reinforcing reading, writing, speaking, and listening behaviors for students who failed to master them in the basic strand.

FOR WHAT OBJECTIVES SHOULD POETRY BE USED?

All, or nearly all, authorities in the field of reading and language arts curricula agree that the teaching of reading, writing, speaking, and listening should be integrated. Hennings (1978) says,

> Because communication is essentially a fluid process with ideas heard and read triggering the production of additional and related ideas to be shared, in designing and structuring language arts programs it is impossible to look upon the traditional language arts areas—thinking, speaking, listening, reading, and writing—as separate curricular experiences. The more effective and logical approach to helping children develop communication skills is to organize a program in which language arts are integrated into the total curriculum and are taught in conjunction with one another and the subject content areas. In an integrated language approach, one aspect of communication flows smoothly and naturally into others with no artificial boundaries separating them. Children talk and write about

thoughts read and heard; they read to find out, enjoy, and share; they talk out before writing about; they share original written work by dramatizing, telling, showing; they work together orally at composing, revising, punctuating, capitalizing, and spelling activities. (p. 3).

The lesson plans for the poems in chapters four and five have been constructed with integration in mind. That is, I have tried to take advantage of the potential of each poem in regard to reading, writing, speaking, and listening activities that are mutually reinforcing in terms of skills development. I have also considered the likely effects of the skill-development activities on students' attitudes toward poetry and tried to avoid activities likely to have a more negative than positive effect.

The poems in chapters four and five and the lesson plans that accompany them should in no way be considered a basic program. They are designed to be supplemental to a basic program, although teachers could easily incorporate some of them into their basic programs. No attempt was made to create a scope and sequence that comprised all the reading and language arts activities children need in the elementary grades. Furthermore, the poems are intended to be only one source for supplementing basic programs.

POETRY AND CURRICULUM OBJECTIVES

Establishing learning objectives should be the starting point for developing the basic reading and language arts curricula. Teachers should decide what students need to learn. They should then design activities and select materials to facilitate that learning. For example, a teacher, after diagnostic observations, might conclude: my students need help in following directions that are given orally, a listening skill. He or she would then find or create materials containing directions. The teacher would instruct the students in purposeful listening, read the directions orally, and guide the students in following the directions until that skill showed improvement. For another example, a teacher might observe his or her students' inability to identify main ideas in printed material. The teacher would assemble stories, poems, essays, or other materials with main ideas, instruct the students in finding main ideas, and provide practice lessons until the skill was mastered.

In the day-to-day world of teaching, the objectives, materials, and activities are usually provided by the authors and publishers of commercial materials: basal reading series, language development series, spelling series, and other published curricula. The authors and editors of these materials coordinate the instructional objectives, materials, and learning activities, as well as determining the grade level(s) at which they are most appropriately used.

The poems in chapters four and five were written with specific reading and language arts objectives in mind, and lesson plans were developed accordingly. Therefore, teachers who use those poems need not be concerned about identifying the objectives the poems can be used to achieve and designing appropriate instructional activities to achieve those objectives. However, for other poems (those recommended in chapter two, for example), that task needs to be done. I wish to assure all readers of this book that the task is not difficult. In addition, it provides a creative outlet for reading and language arts teachers and thereby provides them with a satisfying personal and professional experience, which they are denied when they use materials that come "ready to serve" from a publishing company.

Teachers who want to use poems that have not had instructional apparatus prepared for them should proceed as follows: (1) determine their students' needs (for example, help in identifying main ideas, practice using context clues, experience writing paragraphs, instruction in listening for sequence, practice with oral discussion, assistance in determining author's purpose), (2) select a poem with the instructional potential to meet their students' needs, and (3) construct activities for students to do before, during, and/or after reading or listening to the poems. For example, the following poem, which appears again in chapter four, is filled with descriptive information about a lost cat. An obvious objective would be: The students will recall descriptive information after reading (or listening) to a poem.

Lost and Found

He likes to rub against your legs.
Have you seen my cat?
He sometimes sleeps on windowsills.
He's furry, and he's fat.

His paws look like they're painted on.
They're white; his legs are black.
And you can see when he gets mad
The way he humps his back.

To start his motor, pet him slow.
He'll squeeze his eyes shut tight,
And tuck his legs up under him,
And purr with all his might.

I sure do hope I find him soon.
He's gettin' pretty old,
And I just looked outside for him,
And boy, it's gettin' cold.

He's not supposed to go there,
But I'll bet he's in the park,
Out there huntin' for a bird.
Boy! It's gettin' dark.

He'll get arrested in the park,
No animals allowed.
The police will see him struttin' there
Showin' off, all proud.

Is that the phone? Wait right here.
Maybe he's been found . . .
Hey, guess what? My cat's OK.
They got him at the pound.

As a post-reading or listening experience students might be asked to list as many facts about the cat as they can recall (he likes to rub against your legs, he sleeps on windowsills, he's furry, he's fat, his paws are white, he hunts birds in the park, and so on).

The following poem, "How I Get Cool," appears again in chapter four and describes how one child feels on a very hot day and how that child gets cool. A suitable objective would be: The students will describe how they feel on a very hot (or cold) day; or, the students will write a paragraph (or discuss orally) how they get cool on a hot day or warm on a cold day.

How I Get Cool

What a hot and muggy day.
I think I'm going to roast.
What a drippy, sweaty day.
I feel like buttered toast.

These concrete steps are sizzly-hot.
They're cooking my backside.
The heat is coming through my soles.
My toes are almost fried.

My blouse is sticking to my skin.
My hair is wringing wet.
I drank so much pink lemonade
My stomach's all upset.

The sun is beating on my head.
I have to squint my eyes.
The breeze can't chase the heat away
No matter how it tries.

On days like this, scorchy days,
Here's how I get cool.
I eat three cherry popsicles
And swim in City Pool.

Most poems have the potential to be used for the attainment of more than one instructional objective. After analyzing a poem for its potential, teachers can decide which objective(s) best suits their students' needs.

The process of designing instructional activities (for example, writing an original paragraph, reading orally with good expression, listening for the main idea, creating a different title, discussing personal feelings aroused by the poem) is not a difficult matter. With a little practice teachers have no difficulty deciding upon activities that will be helpful to their students' skills development and that their students will enjoy. Using the poems and lesson plans in chapters four and five should prepare teachers for establishing objectives and designing activities for other poems they use.

Smith and Wortley (in press) experimented with the use of poetry to improve the reading skills of underachieving sixth graders. Analyzing poems for their skill-development potential, determining instructional objectives, and designing instructional activities were integral parts of that study in which poetry was presented to middle grades students as material for their reading skills development. The teaching methodology employed was intended to get students (in this case underachieving sixth graders) to accept and use poetry as a vehicle for reading skills improvement without adversely affecting their attitudes toward reading it. In fact, it was hoped that reading underachievers in the middle grades might even learn to enjoy reading poetry and turn to it for pleasure reading as well as for skills development and practice. The methodology was also intended to make students more aware of their reading skills needs and to encourage them to take a more active role in their reading skills development program.

The teacher who participated in the Smith/Wortley study was a specially trained reading teacher with several years of teaching experience and an interest in children's poetry. She selected fifteen poems and analyzed them for their skills-development potential. The results of that analysis are displayed in the following matrix that appears as figure 1. Other elementary grades teachers would find it useful to analyze in this same way the skills-development potential of poems they plan to use with their classes.

Figure 1
Poem/Reading Skills Matrix

Poem	Reading Orally with Good Expression	Predicting Outcomes	Using Context Clues	Sequencing	Finding Main Idea	Recalling Facts	Imaging	Developing Vocabulary
1	X	X	X		X			X
2			X		X			X
3	X	X	X		X		X	
4	X		X		X			
5	X	X	X	X	X	X	X	X
6		X	X		X		X	X
7		X	X		X	X	X	X
8	X	X	X		X	X	X	
9			X			X		X
10	X			X		X	X	
11	X			X		X	X	
12	X					X		
13	X		X			X	X	
14	X		X			X	X	
15	X	X	X	X				X

In all likelihood the teacher could have identified even more skills that could be taught with the selected poems. However, those on the matrix are widely accepted by reading authorities as important basic skills and were deemed sufficient for the purpose of the study.

The poetry unit Smith and Wortley conducted comprised ten lessons and was taught two days a week for five weeks within fifty-minute class periods. Each of the lessons proceeded as follows:

1. Recalling the content of poems and the skills learned from previous lessons.
2. Identifying the particular reading skill(s) to be learned for the lesson of the day.
3. Demonstrating with a poem how the skill(s) could be learned for that lesson.
4. Reading poems (some orally, some silently) selected for the lesson, and completing appropriate skill development activities.

The activities varied from lesson to lesson depending on the skill(s) to be learned. The activities included context clue analysis; identifying main ideas; making predictions from clues; looking up the definitions of words; constructing lists of rhyming words; adding stanzas; filling in deleted words (clozing); recalling facts and details; recalling the sequences of events; unscrambling scrambled poems (by stanzas); describing mental images; illustrating mental images; and rehearsing, tape recording, and evaluating oral reading.

An evaluative instrument was administered to the students prior to the unit of study and at the conclusion. The results of the two administrations are shown in figure 2.

One more response was solicited from the students in the post-study survey at the conclusion of the unit: "What are three things you learned from the poetry unit we just completed?" This broad, open-ended question rather than a more specific multiple-choice question was employed to avoid leading the students to a response they may not have arrived at on their own. The following are representations of the responses given:

I learned some new words.
Getting pictures in my mind helps.
Put things in the right order.
Poems are fun.
Finding many ideas was fun.
Reading with good expression helps.
It's important to remember facts.
Always think about what you read.

Figure 2
Student Responses to Pre- and Post-Unit Surveys

1. Do you think reading is hard for you, easy for you, or somewhere in between?

	Hard	Easy	Somewhere in Between
Pre:	—	8	23
Post:	—	13	18

2. Do you like to read poems orally?

	Yes	Not sure	No
Pre:	4	15	12
Post:	19	8	4

3. Do you like to read poems silently?

	Yes	Not sure	No
Pre:	20	6	5
Post:	21	5	5

4. Do you like to listen to poems?

	Yes	Not sure	No
Pre:	17	7	7
Post:	23	4	4

5. If you had a choice between reading a poem and a story from your reading book to improve your reading which would you choose?

	Story	Poem
Pre:	17	14
Post:	14	17

6. Would you choose to read poetry for enjoyment?

	Never	Sometimes	Often
Pre:	8	19	4
Post:	7	19	5

The study by Smith and Wortley focused only on reading skills development. However, the poems could have been analyzed for their listening, writing, and speaking skill-development potential as well and appropriate activities designed. To reiterate, identifying instructional objectives and designing activities to attain those objectives are reasonable tasks for teachers who want to enrich their reading and language arts curricula with poetry for which instructional apparatus has not been previously constructed.

REFERENCES

De Haven, Edna P. *Teaching and Learning the Language Arts.* 2nd ed. Boston: Little, Brown, 1983.

Donoghue, Mildred R. *The Child and the English Language Arts.* Dubuque, Iowa: William C. Brown, 1971.

Hennings, Dorothy Grant. *Communication in Action: Dynamic Teaching of the Language Arts.* Chicago: Rand McNally, 1978.

Martin, Bill, Jr. "The Impact of Current Reading Practices on Beginning Readers." In *What Is Reading Doing to the Child?*, ed. Alfred J. Castaldi and Joseph P. Kender. Danville, Ill.: Interstate Printers and Publishers, 1967, pp. 57–63.

Schramm, Wilbur. "How Communication Works," in *Basic Readings in Communication Theory*, ed. C. David Mortensen. New York: Harper & Row, 1973.

Smith, Richard J. & Johnson, Dale D. *Teaching Children to Read.* 2nd ed. Reading, Mass.: Addison-Wesley, 1980.

Smith, Richard J. & Wortley, Dale. "Sixth-Graders Look Closely at Reading Skills and Poetry." *The Middle School Journal* (in press).

CHAPTER 4

Poems for Grades
One, Two, and Three

The poems in this chapter[1] were written to be used with children in the primary grades. They were tested in those grades by teachers from several school districts. The teachers found that the students enjoyed the poems and had no difficulty understanding the messages they contained. In addition, they found that the poems had the potential for teaching or reinforcing many skills included in reading and language arts curricula for the primary grades. In fact, discussions I had with the teachers after their experimentations with the poems were extremely helpful to the construction of the lesson plans that also appear in this chapter.

Most of my discussions with teachers who had used the poems in this chapter and those in chapter five ("Poems for Grades Four, Five, and Six") also disclosed that more than a few of the poems in both chapters are suitable for grades one through six. In some schools, even kindergarten teachers used the poems they felt could be enjoyed by their students and could be useful to the development of certain reading and language arts skills (for example, listening for specific purposes, using context clues to determine word meaning, making predictions, discussing ideas). Therefore, teachers of grades one, two, and three may find poems for their students in chapter five as well as in this chapter, and teachers of grades four, five, and six may also find poems suitable for their students in both chapters.

There is no need to attempt the attainment of all the instructional objectives listed for the following poems, nor is there a need to utilize all the instructional activities. What is helpful for one student or one class may or may not be helpful for another. Some teachers may choose to create their own objectives and activities for the poems. For example, I have chosen to focus on vowel sounds in medial position for phonics instruction because those are the phonic elements children have most difficulty learning. However, the poems could be used as effectively for teaching consonants, blends, or digraphs.

---

[1]The poems in this chapter may only be duplicated for classroom use.

In addition to providing instructional objectives and activities for each of the poems, I have provided a bit of information "About the Poem." From sharing my poems with children I learned that they enjoy hearing about how I happened to write each one. Your students may also enjoy that information. You will notice the information about the poem is required for completion of some of the instructional activities.

GUM'S NO FUN

Every time I chew some gum
My mother says I look as dumb
As some old cow stuck in the mud
Who just stands there and chews her cud.

But Mother doesn't know, you see,
I don't chew gum just for me.
Heavens, no! I do because
I need to exercise my jaws.

About the Poem

I was in a classroom recently, and I heard the teacher tell a boy to throw the gum he was chewing in the wastebasket. Then she said, "If everyone in this class were chewing gum, I would feel like I were teaching a herd of cows chewing their cuds." The students laughed, and so did the teacher.

Instructional Objectives

1. Students will identify words with the short *u* sound in medial position.
2. Students will think of words with short *u* sound and write them in a list.
3. Students will read their lists of short *u* words orally.
4. Students will listen to detect likenesses and differences among items in lists.
5. Students will discover humor in a statement contrary to fact.
6. Students will read orally with good expression.

Instructional Activities

1. Read the poem aloud. Then write the word *cut* on the chalkboard. Next, ask the students to write down all the words in the poem that have the same sound in the middle. Ask them what letter stands for that sound and whether it is the long or short sound of that letter.
2. Ask the students to make a list of other words they know with the short *u* sound in the middle.
3. Have selected or volunteer students read their lists orally while the other students listen for likenesses and differences between the list being read and their list.
4. Ask the students if they think the author really means what he says in the last two lines. Read the lines aloud. Ask them to supply a contrary-to-fact explanation for something they like to do that is not good for them (for example, eat candy, walk outside without shoes on, "forget" their eyeglasses when they come to school, fail to look at a clock at bedtime, watch the late-night TV movie).
5. Ask for volunteers to read the poem orally with good expression.

IF I HAD A WISH

What would I be
If I had a wish?
How about a turtle,
Or maybe a fish?

A bird perhaps,
Or a puppy dog?
Would I be a monkey,
Or a big bullfrog?

An elephant
With a big, long trunk?
Anything—
Except a skunk!

About the Poem

This poem was born in a canoe on a small lake. I was drifting along the bank when I spotted three mud turtles snoozing in the sun on a half-submerged log. I was struck with how much the turtles and I were alike at that moment. When I returned to shore, I wrote down my thoughts.

Instructional Objectives

1. Students will listen for specific information.
2. Students will read to recall specific information.
3. Students will engage in creative thinking and share their thoughts orally.
4. Students will identify the number, kind, and purpose of punctuation marks used.
5. Students will use punctuation marks as signals to guide their oral reading.
6. Students will make inferences about the origin of a poem.

Instructional Activities

1. Read the poem aloud after you tell your students to listen for the one thing the poet would not want to be. Pause before you read the last word in the poem and let your students guess it.
2. Tell your students to read the poem silently (either make copies or project it with an opaque or overhead projector) and then to list from memory all the different things the poet might wish to be. Have them compare their lists.
3. Give your students one minute to write down one thing they might wish to be. Have them share their choices and tell why they wished as they did.
4. Have your students count the number of punctuation marks used in the poem. Then have them tell how many different kinds were used, how many of each kind were used, and what each signalled the reader to do.
5. Ask for volunteers to read the poem orally with good expression, paying close attention to the punctuation marks.
6. Ask your students to speculate about where the author was when he got his idea for this poem. Then share the information "About the Poem" with them.

TELL ME

What's your favorite place of all?
On the playground playing ball?
Or at a motel swimming pool,
Diving, splashing keeping cool?
By your campsite in the park
Toasting weinies in the dark?
In your bedroom leafing through
Books that brought the world to you?
Or in your bed all warm and snuggly,
Snug as any bug in ruggly?
Do you think the woods in fall
Is the finest place of all?
How about a busy street
Filled with cars and tired feet?
I've left a line you'll find below
For you to tell me where you'd go
To find the place that you would call
Your very favorite place of all.

————————————————————!

About the Poem

I was driving across Canada, sometimes camping in a tent, sometimes sleeping in motels when I became lonesome for home and wrote this poem. At the time this poem was written my favorite place was home.

Instructional Objectives

1. Students will listen for specific information.
2. Students will engage in mental imagery as they read.
3. Students will engage in detailed oral description.
4. Students will write about and share their favorite place.
5. Students will interpret figurative language.
6. Students will read orally with good expression.

Instructional Activities

1. Ask the students to listen for the question the author of this poem is asking. Then read the first four lines to the students as they read them silently.
2. Tell the students to read the rest of the poem silently, getting pictures in their minds of all the places mentioned in the poem.
3. Ask for volunteers to describe one of the pictures they formed in their minds as they read. Tell them to describe their mental pictures in detail (sizes, colors, smells, feelings).
4. Have each student fill in the line at the bottom of the poem, and ask for volunteers to share what they wrote. If they do not have individual copies, the poem could be printed on the chalkboard or projected on an overhead.
5. Ask the students to tell what the author means by "Books that brought the world to you."
6. Have seven volunteers each read two lines of the poem in sequence. Then have the whole class read the last four lines chorally.

OUR MOUSE

Whatever happened to the mouse
Who used to live inside our house?

He used to scratch inside the walls
And scoot across the upstairs halls.

That mouse was like a family pet.
You know where he has gone, I'll bet.

I'll bet he's moved out to a farm.
He's in some corn crib doing harm.

Our house was always so darn neat,
He couldn't find enough to eat.

About the Poem

I used to have a small hole in the woodbox behind my cabin. Mice used to crawl in the box to get out of the cold. When the woodbox got falling-apart old, I chopped it up to burn it. As I was chopping it apart, I discovered a nest of twelve field mice living in it. I tipped the box over, but they did not want to leave. I had to chase them out into the woods. Then I wondered where they had gone.

Instructional Objectives

1. Students will read orally with good expression.
2. Students will use context clues to identify word meaning and check their accuracy with a dictionary.
3. Students will identify the unifying question asked in the poem.
4. Students will identify cause-and-effect relationships.
5. Students will engage in creative thinking.
6. Students will write descriptive sentences.
7. Students will identify words with the short *e* sound in medial position.
8. Students will learn that *ea* often has the sound of long *e*.

Instructional Activities

1. Read the poem aloud while the students read it silently. Then have them read it in unison with you one or more times.
2. Write the words *corn crib* on the chalkboard. Tell the students to read the stanza in which they find those words. Then ask them what a crib must be. Ask if they have heard of a baby's crib. Have them suggest a definition as it is used in the poem. Finally, read them the dictionary definition of the word.
3. Tell the students to find the main question the author of the poem asks. Have a volunteer read it.
4. Ask the students to find the stanza that tells why the author thinks the mouse left.
5. Ask the students to think of good names for a pet mouse. Write the names they dictate on the chalkboard.
6. Have each student finish the following stem in two different ways:

   I think the mouse in the poem . . . .

   Have them read their completed sentences aloud.
7. Write the word *jet* on the chalkboard. Point out that the word has a short *e* in the middle. Have them find two words in the poem with short *e* in the middle. Ask them to think of other words with the short *e* sound in the middle. Write those they supply on the chalkboard.
8. Write the words *neat* and *eat* on the chalkboard. Ask the students what they notice about the sound *ea* stands for in both of those words. Ask them to think of other words with the long *e* sound in them. Write their words on the chalkboard and point out that sometimes *ea* stands for the same sound as *ee*.

CAN YOU IMAGINE?

Can you imagine:
A goose reading a newspaper?
Two dogs riding bicycles?
Three ducks wearing raincoats?
Four monkeys shaving?
Five elephants dancing?
Six birds playing with a cat?
Seven rabbits climbing trees?
Eight camels fishing?
I can't!

About the Poem

One day I started thinking about all the things I couldn't imagine. And I couldn't think of anything I couldn't imagine.

Instructional Objectives

1. Students will listen for a specific purpose.
2. Students will engage in mental imagery.
3. Students will describe their mental images orally.
4. Students will engage in creative thinking.
5. Students will write creatively.
6. Students will read what they have written orally with good expression.

Instructional Activities

1. Read the poem to the students slowly. Before you read, tell them to close their eyes and try to get pictures in their minds of what you are reading.
2. Ask each student to select one of the lines in the poem and create a detailed mental picture of it. Have volunteers describe their mental pictures orally (for example, what kinds of birds were playing, what game were they playing, what color(s) was the cat, where were they playing?).
3. Have the students add more items to the poem (nine . . . , ten . . . , eleven . . .). Have them read their additions.
4. Ask each student to select one line from the poem, write a short story about how what is described happened, and illustrate their story. Volunteers may share their stories and pictures with the class.
5. Have the students write the article (or the headline for the article) the goose was reading in the newspaper. Have them read what they write to the class.

HOW ABOUT A LETTER?

How about a letter?
Please write me one today.
How about a letter?
I'm sure you've much to say.

I'm all alone and feeling sad;
I'm lonesome and I'm blue.
How about a letter?
I'm really missing you.

About the Poem

I really like to get a letter from a friend who lives far away. I like letters better than telephone calls. Once I was thinking about a friend I had not seen or heard from for a long time, so I wrote this poem about how I felt.

Instructional Objectives

1. Students will identify words that express feelings and set tone.
2. Students will express the main idea of the poem in an additional title.
3. Students will identify people from whom they would like to receive a letter.
4. Students will write an original letter to a friend or relative.

Instructional Activities

1. Read the poem to the students or have them read it silently. Tell them to listen, or read, to find out how the author was feeling when he wrote the poem.
2. Have the students identify all the words in the poem that told them how the poet felt.
3. Ask the students to create another title for the poem. Have them share their products.
4. Have the students list three people from whom they would like to receive a letter. Have volunteers read their lists.
5. Help the students identify one person (friend, relative, TV personality, athlete, politician) to whom they would like to send a letter. Have them write that person a letter.

MY PUPPY

My puppy can be my very best friend.
He'll lick me and play games for hours on end.
Sometimes he'll kiss me right on the nose,
And try to snuggle under my clothes.

My puppy can also be a big pain,
When he has to go walking out in the rain.
Sometimes he'll chew on a table or chair;
Roll in dirt, and get burrs in his hair.

Sometimes I like my puppy a lot.
Sometimes I do, and sometimes not.
I guess with my puppy it's good and it's bad.
He makes me happy, and he makes me mad.

About the Poem

I used to have a Brittany spaniel named Blitz. He was white with orange spots, floppy ears, and only a stub of a tail. This poem tells how I felt about Blitz.

Instructional Objectives

1. Students will listen to create a mental image.
2. Students will engage in choral reading.
3. Students will write a descriptive paragraph.
4. Students will identify words with short *a, e, i, o,* and *u* in medial position.
5. Students will identify words with long *a, e, i,* and *o* in medial position.

Instructional Activities

1. Tell the students to make a mental picture of the puppy as they listen to you read the poem.
2. Have volunteers describe their mental pictures.
3. Divide the students into groups of three. Assign one stanza to each student for oral reading. After a preparation and rehearsal period have each group read the poem orally, paying careful attention to punctuation marks.
4. Assign each student to write a descriptive paragraph about "My Idea of a Wonderful Pet" and illustrate it if desired. Let all students or volunteers share their paragraphs.
5. Have the students make five lists of words from the poem: words with short *a, e, i, o,* and *u* in medial position.
6. Have the students make four lists of words from the poem: words with long *a, e, i,* and *o* in medial position.

SNOW FUN

What can you do with snow?
Well,
You can blow it,
You can throw it, and
You can make a sled go in it.

I like snow much
Better than rain.
Rain is a pain.
It drowns out the sun.
Rain is a pain, but snow is fun.

About the Poem

I hate rainy days—always have. They are dreary. But snowy days make everything white and bright. You can do a lot with snow, but rain is a pain. I feel sorry for people who live where it rains a lot, but never snows.

Instructional Objectives

1. Students will read orally with good expression.
2. Students will write a paragraph telling about the weather (or season) they like most and least.
3. Students will read their paragraphs aloud.
4. Students will draw a picture of fun in the snow, rain, or sun and write a caption for it.

Instructional Activities

1. Read the poem one sentence at a time. Have the students echo your reading. Then have volunteers read each stanza with good expression.
2. Talk with the students about their most and least favored weather and/or season. Then have them select their most or least favored weather or season and write a paragraph or poem about it.
3. Have all or volunteer students read their written products to the entire class or in small groups.
4. Assign each student to draw a picture of fun in the snow, rain, or sun and caption it or write a sentence about it.

THE BRAVEST THING I KNOW

It has a long, long way to go,
And it must travel very slow.

Danger lies on every side.
There's no way it can catch a ride.

High above, a hungry hawk!
It cannot run. It still must walk.

On the left, a speeding car!
It can't turn back. It's gone too far.

It has no fear of getting lost,
Inch by inch the road is crossed.

What's the bravest thing I know?
A caterpillar on the go!

About the Poem

I was walking along a country road when I spied a furry caterpillar inching its way across the road. The caterpillar was in the middle of the road when a pickup truck came racing by and passed right over it. I had to admire the caterpillar who left the security of the roadside and set out on such a long, unprotected journey. I thought, "What a brave thing to do."

Instructional Objectives

1. Students will make predictions based on limited evidence.
2. Students will learn the dictionary definition of *brave*.
3. Students will make a list of brave people and/or things.
4. Students will explain why the people and/or things on their lists are brave.
5. Students will write a paragraph on the topic of bravery.

Instructional Activities

1. Type or write the poem on an overhead transparency. To begin, show only the title. (This approach can also be accomplished by having the students cover the poem with a sheet of paper and disclosing only parts at a time.) Ask the students to predict what this poem is about. Write some predictions on the chalkboard. Then disclose the poem a stanza at a time, allowing students to retain or change their predictions. For the final stanza, disclose only the first line. Ask the students to write what they think the last line will be. Have them read their written products before you disclose the last line.
2. Ask students to attempt definitions of the word *brave*. Then compare their definitions to a dictionary definition.
3. Have the students make a list of brave things and/or people they know.
4. Arrange the students in groups of three or four to compare their lists and explain why the items on their lists are brave.
5. Assign each student to write a three- or four-sentence paragraph on the topic of "bravery."

GIVE YOURSELF A SUMMER TREAT

Come and buy it, good and sweet.
Give yourself a summer treat.

Good and juicy, plenty nice.
Can't complain about the price.

Step right up, give me your dime.
Come on now, it's coolness time.

Find the seeds and spit 'em out.
That's what fun is all about.

Don't be fooled by all the green.
Inside is red as you have seen.

You want to know what's that I'm sellin'?
Why, folks, I'm sellin' watermelon.

About the Poem

At an outdoor farmers' market a farmer was selling watermelons and watermelon slices. A lot of kids were buying slices and having fun spitting the seeds around, so I bought a slice and joined in the fun.

Instructional Objectives

1. Students will make predictions based on limited evidence.
2. Students will identify the clues that led them to make the correct prediction.
3. Students will identify the words of the speaker.
4. Students will infer words spoken to the speaker.
5. Students will engage in creative thinking.

Instructional Activities

1. Type or print the poem on an overhead transparency. Project the transparency, disclosing only the title. Ask the students to predict what the "summer treat" will be. Write their predictions on the chalkboard. Then disclose the poem one stanza at a time, allowing students to retain or change their predictions. After they see the fourth stanza, insist that they write down their predictions. Then have them read the remainder of the poem silently to check the accuracy of their predictions.
2. Have the students identify (orally or in writing) the clues that pointed to watermelon as the summer treat.
3. Ask the students which lines of the poem are the exact words of a speaker. (They all are.)
4. Direct the students' attention to the final stanza. Ask them to write down the words that must have been spoken to the speaker of the poem (what's that you're sellin'?).
5. Read "About the Poem" to the students. Group them in pairs and assign each pair to create a sign advertising the sale of watermelon slices. Have each pair present its sign to the group.

MONEY AND DOUGHNUTS

Money in my pocket—I'm rich.
Doughnuts in the bakery—I'm hungry.
Money in the baker's pocket—I'm poor.
Doughnuts in me—I'm happy!

About the Poem

One day I had only enough money to pay for my bus ride home, but I spent it on some doughnuts and walked home (four miles).

Instructional Objectives

1. Students will read orally with good expression.
2. Students will engage in creative thinking.

Instructional Activities

1. Read the poem aloud with relatively little expression. Then ask volunteer students to read it with the kind of expression they think each line should have.
2. Write the following stems on the chalkboard. Ask the students to complete each thought, using the pattern from the poem and share their finished products.

> Potato chips in a bag . . . .
> A cool lake to swim in . . . .
> A bus to ride . . . .
> A book to read . . . .
> A supermarket to shop in . . . .

SMALL

Don't be afraid if you're smaller than all.
Lots of tough things are smaller than small.
A dentist's drill is awfully little,
And nothing's tougher than a riddle.

A diamond's small with a big, tough price.
Most everyone's afraid of mice.
Even though they're terribly smallish
Wood ticks make you feel all crawlish.

So if you think you'll never be,
Much bigger than a bumblebee;
Remember, bumblebees can scare
The biggest, roughest, toughest bear.

About the Poem

On a school playground I watched some kids teasing a boy because he was small. They were making a big mistake, I thought. Being tough and being small are two different things.

Instructional Objectives

1. Students will learn the dictionary definition of the word *tough*.
2. Students will listen for a specific purpose.
3. Students will express a main idea in one sentence.
4. Students will identify a coined word.
5. Students will list items in a single category.

Instructional Activities

1. Read the dictionary definitions of the word *tough*.
2. Tell the students to listen as you read the poem for the best definition of the word *tough* as the poet uses it.
3. Ask the students to express the main idea of the poem in one sentence. Help them fashion their responses into a sentence, and write that sentence on the chalkboard.
4. Ask the students to find one word in the poem they think the author probably made up (crawlish).
5. Have the students list all the small, but tough, things the author includes in the poem. Tell them to add one or two of their own.

SNOWFLAKES

Snowflakes, snowflakes falling on the ground.

So softly and gently they never make a _____.
Snowflakes, snowflakes sailing through the breeze.

One sailed up my nose and made me _____.

WHAM

My head is full of words that rhyme;
They pop right out most any time.
I take a pen at school or home,
And, wham! I go and write a poem.
Oh, my gosh, look what I've done.
I've written down another one.

About the Poem

This is a just-for-fun poem. A dog I had once used to chase and bite at snowflakes. Then he would sneeze.

Instructional Objectives

1. Students will use context clues to replace deleted words.
2. Students will read orally with good expression.

Instructional Activity

Read the poem aloud while the students follow along. Pause at each deleted word and ask the students to supply it (sound, sneeze). Then ask volunteers to read all four lines with good expression.

About the Poem

When I read my poems to kids in schools, they often ask, "How can you write so many poems?" This poem is how I answer them.

Instructional Objective

Students will create a couplet.

Instructional Activities

1. Read the information in "About the Poem" to the students. Then read them the poem.
2. Tell them to make a list of words that rhyme with each of the following: eat, scream, hose, sun, night. Then tell them to study the lists and try to write two lines that rhyme and make sense. For example:

> When I cannot see the sun,
> Then I know the day is done.

BRUSHING TEETH IS SUCH A CHORE

Brushing teeth is such a chore.
And isn't it an awful bore?

Up and down. In and out.
Makes a person want to shout,
"I will not do this anymore!
Brushing teeth is such a chore!"

Now listen to my Uncle Fred
Who years ago the same thing said.
"I wish I had my teeth once more.
Eating now is such a chore."

About the Poem

Sometimes I just get tired of doing the things that have to be done every day, like brushing teeth. But having to get cavities drilled every day would be worse. And worst of all would be having no teeth to brush.

Instructional Objectives

1. Students will learn the definition of the word *routine*.
2. Students will discuss and make a list of routine, but necessary, activities in their lives.
3. Students will identify the words of speakers and read them with good expression.

Instructional Activities

1. Write the word *routine* on the chalkboard. Ask the students to attempt a definition. Then read them the dictionary definition.
2. Tell the students to listen to a poem about a routine job everyone has to do. Then read the poem to them.
3. Divide the students into groups of three or four. Assign each group to make a list of routine activities in their lives. Have each group share its list.
4. Tell the students to read the poem once more, this time looking for quotation marks setting off the exact words of speakers. When they find them have volunteers read them the way they think the people would have spoken them.

DON'T CATCH THE FLU

Shivering is what you'll do
If you should go and catch the flu.
And you'll be hot and thirsty, too,
If you should go and catch the flu.

Throwing up is what you'll do
If you should go and catch the flu.
And you'll be dizzy, shaky, too,
If you should go and catch the flu.

It's terrible the things you'll do
If you should go and catch the flu.
And what I say I know is true,
'Cause I just went and caught the flu.

About the Poem

About a year ago the flu came to town. Nearly everybody was either getting the flu or getting over the flu. The poem tells how I felt when I caught it. The first time I read this poem to elementary school students the class had a substitute teacher. The regular teacher was home sick with the flu.

Instructional Objectives

1. Students will learn the meaning of the word *symptom*.
2. Students will list the symptoms of the common cold and other diseases they may have had.
3. Students will listen for a specific purpose.
4. Students will read orally with good expression.
5. Students will write a paragraph on good health habits and read it orally.

Instructional Activities

1. Write the word *symptom* on the chalkboard.
2. Ask the students to attempt a definition before you read them the dictionary definition.
3. Ask the students to list symptoms of the common cold.
4. Tell the students to listen, as you read, for the symptoms of the flu.
5. Ask for volunteers to read individual stanzas orally with good expression.
6. Engage the students in a discussion of good health habits. Then assign each student to write a paragraph on "staying healthy" and read it to the class.

ONCE I DID

Once I drove a racing car
Three hundred miles an hour.
Once I jumped right to the top
Of New York's highest tower.

Once I threw a ball so far
It landed on the moon.
And once I ran to India,
And got back home by noon.

Once I fought a grizzly bear,
And sailed through seven gales.
I'll bet by now you must have guessed
I also tell tall tales.

About the Poem

I watched the students in one classroom having a good time writing tall tales. I thought this poem might encourage other students to have fun writing and sharing their original tall tales.

Instructional Objectives

1. Students will recall the sequence in which events were presented.
2. Students will use context clues to define the word *gale*.
3. Students will engage in mental imagery.
4. Students will give an oral description.
5. Students will think creatively.

Instructional Activities

1. Have the students read the poem silently, just for fun.
2. Have the students read the poem a second time for the purpose of noticing the sequence in which the events are presented. Then ask them to list the events as they were presented.
3. Ask the students to tell how context clues disclose the meaning of the word *gale*.
4. Have each student imagine one of the events pictured as a cartoon. Ask volunteers to describe their pictures. Some may want to draw their cartoons.
5. Assign each student to write a tall tale and read it to the class.

THE CHRISTMAS PRESENT

What's here in this package
Right under the tree?
The tag says "Juanita."
Juanita, that's me.

I'll bet this is perfume
To make me smell nice.
I know it! It's perfume!
I'll smell just like spice.

No sense in my waiting.
Come here to my nose.
I don't smell a thing.
Oh, no! It's just clothes.

About the Poem

Like Juanita in the poem, my children always liked to get toys and games for presents, not new clothes. However, some students who read this poem said they would rather have new clothes than perfume. People are different, but I agree with Juanita.

Instructional Objectives

1. Students will predict outcomes.
2. Students will make inferences.
3. Students will recall specific information.
4. Students will identify the main idea.
5. Students will attend to punctuation marks to read with expression.
6. Students will write creatively.

Instructional Activities

1. Have the students read only the first two stanzas. Then ask them to guess what Juanita's present is.
2. After they read the final stanza ask the students how Juanita knew the present was clothes besides the fact that the package had no smell.
3. Ask the students to recall which word rhymed with *nice*.
4. Have each student supply another title for this poem. Let the class vote on the best title.
5. Ask for volunteers to read the poem orally. Remind them to use the punctuation marks to help them read with good expression.
6. Assign the students to write Juanita's thank-you note for the present. They will have to decide who gave her the present.

HOW I GET COOL

What a hot and muggy day.
I think I'm going to roast.
What a drippy, sweaty day.
I feel like buttered toast.

These concrete steps are sizzly-hot.
They're cooking my backside.
The heat is coming through my soles.
My toes are almost fried.

My blouse is sticking to my skin.
My hair is wringing wet.
I drank so much pink lemonade
My stomach's all upset.

The sun is beating on my head.
I have to squint my eyes.
The breeze can't chase the heat away
No matter how it tries.

On days like this, scorchy days,
Here's how I get cool.
I eat three cherry popsicles
And swim in City Pool.

About the Poem

The day I wrote this poem the temperature was ninety-two degrees and the humidity was 85 percent. Two little girls near our house had opened up a lemonade stand. One was eating a popsicle. I was sure they had been drinking their lemonade, and I bet they would be heading for the pool when someone was able to take them there.

Instructional Objectives

1. Students will listen for specific information.
2. Students will discuss ways to stay cool.
3. Students will identify descriptive words.
4. Students will identify words with short and long vowel sounds.

Instructional Activities

1. Read the poem to the students after you tell them to listen to find out how the narrator gets cool.
2. Divide the students into groups of three and assign each group to produce a list of "ways to stay cool on scorchy days."
3. Have the students identify all words or word groups in the poem that give the feeling of "hot."
4. Have the students identify words with short and long vowel sounds.

ALL ALONE? NOT QUITE!

If I had a space ship
I'd blast off from the crowds,
Sail into the clear, blue sky,
Look down upon the clouds.

I'd aim my ship higher yet,
And head right for the stars,
Blast right through the Milky Way—
There's Jupiter, here's Mars.

Here I am, just me alone,
Way up here in space.
Oh, my gosh! What's that I see?
A Martian kid's green face.

About the Poem

Whenever astronauts blast off, many of us would like to go along. Imagine how peaceful it must seem way up in space, all alone . . . maybe!

Instructional Objectives

1. Students will listen for main idea.
2. Students will identify the author's purpose.
3. Students will formulate original questions.
4. Students will create and present a dramatization.

Instructional Activities

1. Read the poem aloud to the students. Ask them to tell what happened in their own words.
2. Write the following on the chalkboard: patriotic, humorous, informative. Ask the students which one fits this poem best. Have them explain their answers.
3. Divide the students into groups of three. Tell each group to write down four questions they think a kid from Mars would ask them. (Yes-No questions are not allowed.) Then have each group interview one student from another group as if they were appearing on a Martian show. You may wish to have the students write original Martian commercials and tape record the presentations.

LOST AND FOUND

He likes to rub against your legs.
Have you seen my cat?
He sometimes sleeps on windowsills.
He's furry, and he's fat.

His paws look like they're painted on.
They're white; his legs are black.
And you can see when he gets mad
The way he humps his back.

To start his motor, pet him slow.
He'll squeeze his eyes shut tight,
And tuck his legs up under him,
And purr with all his might.

I sure do hope I find him soon.
He's gettin' pretty old,
And I just looked outside for him,
And, boy, it's gettin' cold.

He's not supposed to go there,
But I'll bet he's in the park,
Out there huntin' for a bird.
Boy! It's gettin' dark.

He'll get arrested in the park,
No animals allowed.
The police will see him struttin' there
Showin' off, all proud.

Is that the phone? Wait right here.
Maybe he's been found . . .
Hey, guess what? My cat's OK.
They got him at the pound.

About the Poem

This is the last poem I wrote for this book. I had written poems about chipmunks, raccoons, bears, dogs, and other animals, but I did not have any about cats. So I wrote this one. The cat in the poem is imaginary.

Instructional Objectives

1. Students will learn the definition of the word *pound* as an enclosed place for stray animals.
2. Students will engage in mental imagery while listening.
3. Students will read for the purpose of recalling details.
4. Students will read orally with good expression.
5. Students will identify contractions in the poem.
6. Students will learn the format for writing classified advertisements.
7. Students will create a classified advertisement for a lost cat.
8. Students will create and read the dialogue that might take place between the narrator and the keeper of the pound.

Instructional Activities

1. Write the word *pound* on the chalkboard. Then read the dictionary definition of *pound* as an enclosed place for stray animals. Ask students to volunteer any experiences they might have had with animal pounds.
2. Tell the students to try to get a mental picture of the lost cat as you read the poem to them.
3. Have the students read the poem silently for the purpose of recalling details about the cat. After they have read, ask them to write down (or volunteer orally) as many details about the cat as they can remember.
4. Ask for volunteers to read their favorite stanza aloud with good expression.
5. Teach the students what a contraction is. Then have them find all the contractions in the poem.
6. Read several lost-and-found ads to the students, and talk about the kind of information they contain. Then divide the students into pairs and have each pair create a classified ad for the cat in the poem. Have them give the cat a name and read their products aloud.
7. Divide the students into pairs again and have them write and read the dialogue that might take place between the narrator and the keeper of the pound when the narrator picks up the cat.

CHAPTER 5

Poems for Grades Four, Five, and Six

The poems in this chapter[1] were written to be used with fourth, fifth, and sixth graders. I have found students in these grades to be very receptive to poetry, so writing poems for them was a pleasant activity. I had many happy times visiting schools and sharing these poems with this age group.

The poems were tested with students from these three grades by teachers from several school districts. They found the poems well suited to the interests and abilities of fourth, fifth, and sixth graders. The teachers gave me many ideas for how the poems could be used to attain a variety of reading and language arts curriculum objectives for the intermediate grades. I have drawn upon their suggestions in writing the lesson plans that accompany the poems. These same teachers also used some of the poems in chapter four successfully with their fourth, fifth, and sixth graders and commented that some of the poems in this chapter were suitable for students in the primary grades as well. Therefore, the titles of chapter four and this chapter should be interpreted loosely.

I will say for this chapter what I said for chapter four: the instructional objectives and activities in the lesson plan accompanying each poem should be modified to meet the needs of a particular student, small group, or entire class. Teachers should use all, some, or none of the plans included according to their professional judgment. Teachers who have read the poems and the plans as they appear in this chapter have pointed out other objectives and other kinds of instructional activities that could have been selected and designed for them. So the poems have instructional potential additional to that tapped by the lesson plans I created, and some teachers may want to tap that additional potential by devising their own lesson plans.

For each poem in this chapter I included a little information "About the Poem" as I did for the poems in chapter four because the students with whom the poems have been tested enjoyed a personal note relative to the origins of the poems.

---

[1] The poems in this chapter may only be duplicated for classroom use.

PROLOGUE

Chipmunks love a woodpile
More than bears are fond of honey.
They even love a woodpile
More than rich folks love their money.

THE ACTOR

A chipmunk on a pile of oak,
His nose all twitchy-shiny;
Figurin' he's king of all,
Forgettin' he's so tiny.

"Hey," he says, "You can't catch me.
These logs are filled with spaces
Just big enough for me to find
And use for hidin' places."

He boasted on and even grinned,
Just teasin' me and teasin',
Scoldin' me and actin' smart.
I didn't know his reason.

For I had never bothered him,
Don't even own a gun.
I guess that he was feelin' tough
And out to have some fun.

I tried to warn him, struttin' there
Arrogant and fat,
Keepin' beady eyes on me,
But not the neighbor's cat.

About the Poem

I have a cabin with a woodpile out back. Chipmunks love to play on and in the pile of logs. They get very bold and saucy if someone is watching them, which I often do. One day I saw the neighbor's big, golden-colored cat walking away from the woodpile with a chipmunk by the neck. I wondered if the poor chipmunk had been more intent on showing off for an imagined observer than watching out for "Goldie."

Instructional Objectives

1. Students will identify the main idea.
2. Students will recall facts.
3. Students will identify comparison relationships.
4. Students will make inferences.
5. Students will write descriptive sentences.
6. Students will read orally with good expression.

Instructional Activities

1. Have the students read the poem and take the following comprehension test.
   a. The chipmunk was
      (a) shot
      (b) caught in a trap
      (c) caught by a cat
   b. Which of the following best fits the main idea of this poem?
      (a) Know thine enemy.
      (b) A penny saved is a penny earned.
      (c) Don't count your chickens before they hatch.
   c. Which of the following best fits the chipmunk?
      (a) angry
      (b) show off
      (c) patriotic
   d. Chipmunks' love for a woodpile is compared to
      (a) bears' fondness for honey
      (b) the neighbors' love for their cat
      (c) the author's love for guns
   e. If the author had tried to catch him, the chipmunk would have
      (a) hidden in a space in a log
      (b) climbed a nearby tree
      (c) run away from the woodpile
   f. How did the author feel when he was watching the chipmunk?
      (a) fearful
      (b) amused
      (c) angry
2. Have your students tell this story in writing in no more than three
   sentences. Have them read their sentences aloud.
3. Ask for volunteers to read a stanza the way the author would probably
   read it.
4. Ask your students how they think the author got the idea for this poem.
   Then read them "About the Poem."

WHAT HAPPENED?

What happened to our yard last night?
Come here and look around.
Why, you can see all kinds of things
Lying on the ground.

Sidewalk full of half-drowned worms,
Street all muddy-wet,
Grass all strewn with parts of trees,
Garbage cans upset.

Water's dripping everywhere—
Sliding from green leaves,
Gliding down slick window panes,
Slipping off the eaves.

Trickling down the driveway,
Two streams of water meet,
And search beneath some leaves and twigs
Before they find the street.

I know what's happened to our yard.
It's had a bath, I'll bet.
All the dirt's still in the tub,
And the water's not out yet.

About the Poem

I got the idea for this poem as I was watching rainwater running down our driveway and into the storm sewer, carrying along leaves and small twigs. The scene reminded me of water running down a bathtub drain.

Instructional Objectives

1. Students will make predictions based on limited information.
2. Students will create mental images as they read.
3. Students will discuss their mental images.
4. Students will identify the letter sound that provides the prominent alliteration in the poem.
5. Students will write a descriptive paragraph.
6. Students will read their written products aloud.

Instructional Activities

1. Read the first stanza to your students and ask them to speculate about "what happened."
2. Have your students read the rest of the poem silently to test their speculations.
3. Ask your students to tell which stanza gave them the clearest mental picture.
4. Write the word *alliteration* on the chalkboard, explain its meaning, and have the students find examples of it in the poem.
5. Have your students write a paragraph describing some area they are familiar with after a rain or snow storm, in the early morning, at noon, in the evening, or at night. Encourage them to use vivid verbs and adjectives. Have them read their descriptions aloud.

BEHIND MY SMILE

If you think I'm never sad,
I'll tell you what let's do.
You be me for just one day,
And I'll in turn be you.

You just hop inside of me,
And be me for awhile.
Think my thoughts, and do my jobs;
Find out what makes me smile.

By the way, while you are me
As one day passes by,
You'll also learn behind my smile
I sometimes want to cry.

About the Poem

In this poem I tried to put into words something almost everyone has felt at one time or another. Other people expect us to be happy and smiling as we go about our business, so we smile and act happy. But sometimes our smiles are masks that hide our true feelings.

Instructional Objectives

1. Students will make content predictions based on the title.
2. Students will write the central thought of a poem in their own words.
3. Students will discuss personal experiences with hiding their feelings.
4. Students will write a position statement.

Instructional Activities

1. Read the title of the poem to the students. Ask them to tell what they think the message of the poem will be.
2. Tell them to read the poem silently and write the main idea in their own words. Ask them to share their products.
3. Ask for volunteers to tell about times when they hid or tried to hide their feelings.
4. Write the following statements on the chalkboard:

> People should hide their true feelings sometimes.
> People should never hide their true feelings.

Tell the students to select one and write a paragraph or two explaining their position.

GERALDINE JACKSON

For a kid who loves to eat
Geraldine Jackson can't be beat.
All considered, bite for bite,

She has a monstrous _____.
Smack!

She always, always cleans her plate.
For dinner time she's never late.
Neither her mother nor her pop

Ever tells her, "Time to _____."
Burp!

Once she ate three lemon pies.
I don't know how she closed her eyes.
Drank a milk shake so darn thick

Even Geraldine got _____.
Ugh!

I saw her eat a whole fried chicken,
And then she even got to lickin'
Off the bones 'til they were bare.

Wouldn't you think her clothes would _____?
Rip!

Geraldine just makes me cry.
Yes, I cry. Do you know why?
Geraldine can eat like that

And never gain an ounce of _____.
Sob!

About the Poem

One summer I went on a diet and felt hungry all the time. I used to watch all the kids in our neighborhood eating ice cream, candy, and other good things and staying thin. I wished I could be like them, especially like one girl who was skinny and ate all the time.

Instructional Objectives

1. Students will use context clues to complete sentences.
2. Students will read orally with good expression.
3. Students will create a title for the poem.
4. Students will engage in mental imagery and write a descriptive paragraph.

Instructional Activities

1. Read the poem to the students, pausing to let them say the deleted words (appetite, stop, sick, tear, fat).
2. Ask for volunteers to read their favorite stanzas orally.
3. Tell the students to write down what they think would be another good title for the poem. Have them share their products. Then read them "About the Poem."
4. Have the students try to imagine other things about Geraldine (how she looks, how she dresses, what sports she likes) and write a paragraph describing Geraldine.

SUMMER CAMP

Summer camp is such a joy,
Games and sports for girl and boy.

Summer camp is so much fun,
All day long just swim and run.

Summer camp is so delightful,
No one here's the least bit spiteful.

Summer camp's not hard to take,
Canoe and fish in Big Bass Lake.

If summer camp is such a picnic,
How come I feel so darn homesicknic?

About the Poem

One of the hazards of going away from home is getting homesick. I always thought the word *homesick* was very descriptive; when I first went to summer camp, I really learned what the word meant. I got so homesick I even tried to run away. That was in 1945. I never went to summer camp again.

Instructional Objectives

1. Students will identify a manufactured word.
2. Students will share personal experiences orally.
3. Students will identify words with suffixes.
4. Students will supply words with suffixes.
5. Students will write creatively.

Instructional Activities

1. Tell the students to listen as you read the poem. Then ask them which word was made up by the poet.
2. Ask volunteers to share their personal experiences with homesickness and/or summer camp.
3. Remind students what a suffix is, and have them identify the two words with the same suffix.
4. Write the following suffixes on the chalkboard: *-ful, -ness, -er,* and *-est.* Ask them to think of words with those suffixes.
5. Tell the students to imagine they are at summer camp. Have them write a letter to a friend or relative telling what they are doing and how they feel.

MY SCARY BOOK

Take a _____ inside this book
If you think you _____.
For in this book, this very book,
Scary things are there.

You'll meet a beast that's running loose.
It broke out of its cage.
And there's a monster in this book

On almost every _____.

My poem about a wicked _____
Will surely make you shiver.
She catches little girls and boys

And makes them eat raw _____.

How about a creature who

Comes to your house one _____,

And _____ right into bed with you
When you turn out the light.

I really cannot tell you more.
Please put this on a shelf.
I've written down such terrible stuff

I've even _____ _____.

About the Poem

I wrote this poem for a class of fifth graders for Halloween. It didn't scare them much, but they enjoyed reading it with a scary expression.

Instructional Objectives

1. Students will use context clues to complete sentences.
2. Students will determine author's purpose.
3. Students will read orally with good expression.
4. Students will make a list of similar things.
5. Students will engage in creative thinking.
6. Students will create a story outline.

Instructional Activities

1. Tell the students to read the poem silently and to fill in deleted words (look, dare, page, witch, liver, night, crawls or creeps, scared myself).
2. Have the students answer the following question and defend their answers:

    The poet wanted people who read his poem to
    a. be scared
    b. smile
    c. cry
    d. be angry

3. Ask volunteers to select their favorite stanzas and read them orally.
4. Have the students make a list of other scary things that might be in this book.
5. Have the students create good titles for scary books, draw a picture for the cover of a scary book, or draw a picture of one of the scary things mentioned in the poem.
6. Arrange students in pairs. Ask each pair to create an outline (characters, setting, plot) for a scary story. Have each pair share its outline.

THE WOODS AT NIGHT

The woods at night are not the same
As they are in the day.
At night the little animals
All come out to play.

A raccoon sleeping in the shade
Feels the sun go down.
He yawns and stretches, sniffs the air,
And thinks about "downtown."

Downtown for him is your campsite,
Strewn with tasty crumbs.
He puts his nose down to
The ground and signals to his chums.

In twos or threes they start their trek;
The forest comes alive.
Sniffing, grunting they advance.
In minutes they arrive.

They see you sitting by your fire,
But you don't know they're there.
You're bigger, stronger, smarter too,
But they don't even care.

They know when they step into view
You'll run. They know you'll scamper.
'Cause you're no different from the rest.
You're just another camper.

About the Poem

A year ago I pitched a tent and camped on Madelline Island in Lake Superior. The island is right off the tip of Bayfield, Wisconsin. The first night three huge raccoons came calling and refused to be shooed away. One even tried to open my cooler. That night I slept in my pickup truck. The raccoons were gone in the morning and so was all the food from supper that I had not put back in the cooler.

Instructional Objectives

1. Students will predict content from the title.
2. Students will identify the main idea.
3. Students will locate a specific place on a map.
4. Students will identify compound words.
5. Students will identify a cause-and-effect relationship.
6. Students will write dialogue.
7. Students will read their creative writing orally with good expression.

Instructional Activities

1. Write the title of the poem on the chalkboard. Have the students predict what a poem with that title might be about. Then tell them it is about raccoons, and have volunteers tell what they know about raccoons.
2. Have the students read the poem silently and suggest a more descriptive title based on the content of the poem.
3. Read "About the Poem" to the students, provide a map of Wisconsin, and help them find Madelline Island on it.
4. Ask the students to find the two compound words in the poem. Have them volunteer other compound words with which they are familiar.
5. Have the students find a cause-and-effect relationship in the poem.
6. Divide the students into groups of three. Assign each group to write the dialogue that might occur between three raccoons before, during, and after their visit to a campsite. Have each group present its product to the class.

TOMORROW

Whatever happened to yesterday?
Yesterday I meant to say,
"I'm sorry that I was so bad.
I'm sorry that I made you sad."

Today I plan to make amends.
Today I hope that we'll be friends.
But now I feel ashamed and blue.
I really cannot talk to you.

Tomorrow for sure, wait and see.
Friends, again, you and me.
But tomorrow I should write that letter!
Day after tomorrow will be much better.

About the Poem

Two words that are very hard for some people to say are, "I'm sorry." I wrote this poem for all the people who have lost friends because they did not say those two little words.

Instructional Objectives

1. Students will listen for a specific purpose.
2. Students will paraphrase complex ideas.
3. Students will write a paragraph for a given topic sentence.

Instructional Activities

1. Tell the students to listen as you read the poem to discover the message the poet is sending. Read the poem aloud twice.
2. Engage the students in an open discussion about the message in the poem. Ask them: What is the poet trying to tell us? Then read them "About the Poem."
3. Write the following topic sentence on the chalkboard and have the students write a paragraph for it:

   A true friend should not be afraid to say, "I'm sorry."

LISTENING

Off and on all night long
I listened to that lonely song.

All the other birds at rest,
Sound asleep in bush or nest.
Cottage lights no longer gleaming,
Folks asleep, drifting, dreaming.
Through the pines two deer slipped past
The soft-light shafts the moon had cast.

"All alone. Answer me.
Answer me. Answer me."

Through the forest dark and still
The lonely call of "whip-poor-will."

About the Poem

Whip-poor-wills are birds that sing at night. Many times I have fallen asleep listening to their call. One of the most beautiful sounds I know is a chorus of three or four of these birds singing together.

Instructional Objectives

1. Students will make predictions based on context clues.
2. Students will draw inferences.
3. Students will learn about whip-poor-wills.

Instructional Activities

1. Read the first stanza of the poem orally and ask the students what they think that "lonely song" is. Read the first two lines of the second stanza and ask them again.
2. Have the students read the rest of the second stanza silently for the purpose of determining the setting for the poem.
3. Tell the students to read the remainder of the poem. Then ask for volunteers to read lines nine and ten aloud.
4. Read the students an encyclopedia entry for whip-poor-will.

FEELING GOOD—FEELING BAD

What is it makes you feel so swell
That you could just jump up and yell,
"I'm happy that I'm who I am.
My life tastes good as thick, sweet jam"?

What is it makes you feel so sad
That inside you feel awful bad
'Cause you are you and have to stay
Inside of you both night and day?

If you could find just which is which,
And rearrange your life a twitch,
You might avoid what makes you sad,
Do only things that make you glad.

It may not happen right away,
But in the future you might say,
"I'm always glad I'm who I am.
My life tastes good as thick, sweet jam."

About the Poem

I really do not believe that anyone can be happy all the time, but I think most people can work toward that goal—even if they never reach it. The secret to being happy is in believing that you can be.

Instructional Objectives

1. Students will listen to determine tone.
2. Students will read orally with good expression.
3. Students will identify comparison relationships.
4. Students will categorize items.
5. Students will make judgments based on logic and explain them orally.

Instructional Activities

1. Write the words *optimistic* and *pessimistic* on the chalkboard. Help the students arrive at a definition for each. Then tell them to listen as you read to discover which word fits the poem better.
2. Ask for volunteers to read stanzas one and two orally with expression that fits the content of each.
3. Ask the students what two unlike things are being likened in the poem (life and jam). Have them make a list of other things to which life might be compared (for example, life tastes good as hot soup on a cold day) and share their lists.
4. Have the students make one list of things in their lives that make them happy and one list of things that make them sad. Have them explain how one or more of the things in their sad list might be eliminated.

WHO'S THERE?

What an awful, terrible scary night.
I'd like to get up and turn on the light;
But my brother, Bill, would call me a chicken,
And Pa might even give me a lickin'.

Oh, why did I watch that late night movie?
With all the lights on it seemed really groovy
To stay up and watch that great double feature,
Featurin' Fin Man, the undersea creature.

But now in the dark I hear water drippin'
And fin feet slitherin', slidin', and slippin'
Up through the bathtub, straight from the sea.
I just know it's old Fin Man comin' for me.

My hands are icy; so are my feet.
Thinkin' of Fin Man makes my heart skip a beat.
I'm so scared I'm drippin' tears on my pillow,
Just a lubberin', slubberin' old weepin' willow.

Why don't he come? Why is he stallin'?
He must have heard me alone in here bawlin'.
I hope old Fin Man's caught in the drain,
Sloshin' and ploshin', turnin' to rain.

I just can't take lyin' here anymore.
I just got to open that bathroom door.
There's water runnin' and light underneath—
Oh, hi, Bill. Watcha doin'? Brushin' your teeth?

About the Poem

I wrote this poem for all the people who watch scary movies before
bedtime and then wish they hadn't.

Instructional Objectives
1. Students will evaluate the poem.
2. Students will read to recall specific information.
3. Students will identify poetic devices.
4. Students will make decisions in a group.
5. Students will write creatively.
6. Students will present their written products orally.

Instructional Activities
1. Read the poem to the students. Then ask them to tell what they did or did not like about it.
2. Tell the students to read the poem silently paying careful attention to details. Then give them the following test.
   a. The speaker's brother's name was
      (a) Pete   (b) Dick   (c) Bill
   b. The speaker called his father
      (a) Pop   (b) Pa   (c) Dad
   c. How many movies did the speaker watch?
      (a) one   (b) two   (c) three
   d. The speaker feared Fin Man was coming through the
      (a) bathtub   (b) sink   (c) laundry tub
   e. What word in the poem rhymed with the work *rain?*
      (a) brain   (b) pain   (c) drain
   f. The speaker compares himself to a
      (a) tree   (b) monster   (c) river
   g. What was Bill doing?
      (a) washing his hands   (b) taking a bath   (c) brushing his teeth
3. Write the word *alliteration* on the chalkboard, explain its meaning, and have the students find examples of it in the poem.
4. Ask the students to explain why the author used *in'* instead of *ing* on the ends of the speaker's words.
5. Write the word *metaphor* on the chalkboard, define it, and have the students find one in the poem (the speaker compares himself to a weeping willow).
6. Divide the students into groups of three. Have each group complete one of the following projects and present the product to the class.
   a. Write and illustrate a newspaper advertisement for a Fin Man movie.
   b. Write an introduction for a Fin Man movie to be delivered by Mad Murphy, host of Channel 13's Late Nite Movie.
   c. Create several movie monsters and tell the names of the movies in which they are featured.
   d. Write an interview between the actor who plays the part of Fin Man and a TV talk show host.

A LETTER IS BETTER

Nothing is better than to get a letter
From someone you really miss.
Sometimes a letter is really much better
Than a handshake or even a kiss.

Handshakes and kisses are given and gone;
They touch you and quickly take flight.
Handshakes and kisses don't last very long, and
You can't put them under your pillow at night.

DUCK WALK

Nothing's slicker than a duck
Afloat upon the water.
But when it walks along the shore,
It really shouldn't oughter.

About the Poem

I have heard that some people sleep with their love letters under their pillow. I guess that is a good idea—if you don't have too many love letters.

Instructional Objective

Students will write creatively.

Instructional Activity

Have each student write a letter he or she would like to receive. Have them read their products orally.

About the Poem

One of my favorite poets is Ogden Nash. This is the kind of silly poems he wrote.

Instructional Objectives

1. Students will identify author's purpose.
2. Students will identify elements that create humor.
3. Students will assign adverbs to activities.
4. Students will describe an activity in writing.

Instructional Activities

1. Tell the students to read the poem to discover whether it is humorous or serious.
2. Ask the students to identify the elements that make the poem humorous (the title, the subject, the mental picture produced, the word *oughter*). Explain the function of adverbs.
3. Have the students assign adverbs to a swimming duck (the duck swam smoothly, gracefully, quietly, beautifully) and to a walking duck (the duck walked along the shore clumsily, awkwardly, uncertainly).
4. Have each student describe in writing the bodily movements that occur when walking. Have them read their products orally.

SYMPATHY

A truck rolled by, its load piled high.
"My tires hurt," it pouted.
I limped along, my own song gone.
"You're not alone!" I shouted.

FALL

Warm pumpkin pie—fall's in my mouth.
I can hear fall—geese flying south.
Trees with gold leaves—fall's in my eye.
The part I like best is—warm pumpkin pie.

WINTER

What's good about winter:
Trees without leaves?
Snow to be shoveled?
Cars that won't start?
Cold wind that hurts?
Nope!
Warm, flannel shirts.

About the Poem

On my walk home from work one night I saw the truck in the poem. I suppose trucks do not get tired, but *it* looked like *I* felt.

Instructional Objectives

1. Students will identify personification.
2. Students will identify figurative language.

Instructional Activities

1. Read the students "About the Poem." Then read the poem to them.
2. Show the poem to the students and have them find an example of personification and an example of figurative language.

About the Poems

Poems about the seasons of the year are easy and fun to write. Everybody should try to write one.

Instructional Objective

Students will write an original poem.

Instructional Activity

Let the students read both poems silently. Then engage them in a discussion about things they see, hear, taste, and feel in the spring and summer. Tell them to use the same patterns to write original poems entitled "Spring" and "Summer." Assure them that their poems need not rhyme.

IMAGINING BY THE SEA

I know that I will always like
To walk beside the sea,
Imagining I'm lots of things
That I can never be.

Imagining that I'm a wave
Washing this white beach,
Stretching water fingers out
As far as they will reach.

Imagining that I'm a shark,
The biggest ever seen;
Scaring fishes left and right,
'Cause I'm so hungry-mean.

Imagining that I'm a gull
Resting on a piling, then
Flapping up above the waves,
Fishing while I'm flying.

Imagining that I'm a fish,
A dolphin with a snout,
Sewing up an ocean path
By dipping in and out.

Imagining I'm anything
That's part of this old sea,
Until a sand burr bites my toe.
And then I know I'm me.

About the Poem

About one and one-half hours flying time out of Miami, on the island of Abaco, is a lovely beach called Treasure Cay Beach. The sand is white, the waves are gentle, and dolphins occasionally swim off the beach during the early morning hours. This is my favorite vacation spot. The poem tells how I feel as I walk along the three-mile-long beach.

Instructional Objectives

1. Students will listen for comparison relationships.
2. Students will identify unusually used adjectives.
3. Students will identify figurative language.
4. Students will locate Treasure Cay on a map.
5. Students will conduct research on the country of the Bahamas.
6. Students will engage in creative thinking and writing.

Instructional Activities

1. Before reading the poem to the students instruct them to listen for the comparison relationships the poet establishes between himself and sea things. Then read the poem and ask students to identify the comparisons that are made.
2. Review the definition of an adjective. Ask the students to find two unusually used adjectives (water, hungry-mean).
3. Write the following on the chalkboard: "The moon, riding across the sky on the backs of clouds." Explain that this is figurative language. Ask the students to find an example of figurative language in the poem.
4. On a map of the Bahama Islands, have the students find, or show them, the location of Abaco Island and Treasure Cay.
5. Ask for one or more volunteers to do some research on the Bahama Islands or read them an encyclopedia entry.
6. Divide the class into groups of three or four. Let each group choose one of the following projects, complete it, and present it to the class.
   a. Create a travel brochure recommending a trip to the Bahama Islands. Be sure to use descriptive adjectives and vivid verbs.
   b. Create a television or radio commercial recommending the Bahama Islands for a vacation. Be sure to use descriptive adjectives and vivid words.
   You may want to provide travel brochures for them to use as references.

NIGHT SOLDIER

He takes his post at time of moon
While others take their nests.
His song is soothing to their sleep,
Heads tucked against their breasts.

He guards the fort while others sleep,
This soldier of the night;
Singing out that "all-is-well"
Until the morning's light.

His throat must ache from so much song,
He never slows his trill.
This sleepless bird, insomniac,
This restless whip-poor-will.

About the Poem

Whip-poor-wills are my favorite bird. They sing through the night and provide a comforting sound from the dark, pine forest.

Instructional Objectives

1. Students will listen for the main idea.
2. Students will express the main idea in their own words in writing.
3. Students will use context clues to define words.
4. Students will identify personification and figures of speech.
5. Students will read orally with good expression.

Instructional Activities

1. Tell the students to listen as you read the poem for the main idea or central thought in the poem. Read it twice.
2. Have the students read the poem silently and write the main idea of the poem in one or two complete sentences.
3. Call the students' attention to the fact that the author does not use the word *bird* until the second to last line. Ask them how they knew it was about birds before that. Then ask them to use context clues to define *insomniac*. Read them a dictionary definition to check their accuracy.
4. Explain personification and figure of speech. Then have the students find examples of both in the poem.
5. Ask for volunteers to read their favorite stanzas orally.
   Ask someone who has heard a whip-poor-will to read the words "all-is-well" in the second stanza as a whip-poor-will would sing them.

When they're new, they're sure no treat,
But broken-in, they can't be beat.

The problem's solved. With them I see
What was before a blur to me.

It brightens up my life each night.
Thank heavens for Ben Franklin's kite.

You tell me what I need to know
To get to where I want to go.

AH, CHOO!

Don't make a sound. Sit very still.
He's coming closer. See if he will
Come right to our picnic table.
I think he will if you are able
To stop the sneeze that's in your nose.
Oh, no! There it goes!
"Ah, choo! Ah, choo!"
You noisy girl.
You sneezed away that curious squirrel.

About the Poems

These are just-for-fun couplets. Everyone should try writing one.

Instructional Objective

Students will use context clues to identify the subject.

Instructional Activity

Have the students title each couplet (e.g., Shoes or Boots, Eyeglasses, Electricity, Map).

About the Poem

The picnic table was in our backyard. The sneezer was my son, but *son* does not rhyme with *squirrel*. Actually the animal was a gopher, but *gopher* doesn't rhyme with any word I know except *loafer*. Sometimes poets have to stretch the truth a little.

Instructional Objectives

1. Students will read orally with good expression.
2. Students will construct lists of rhyming words.
3. Students will write and read orally an original couplet.

Instructional Activities

1. Ask the students to study the poem for the purpose of reading it orally with good expression. Then let volunteers try it.
2. Read the students "About the Poem." Ask them to think of words that rhyme with *gopher* and *boy*.
3. Have the students try writing a couplet rhyming *gopher* and *loafer* (That lazy gopher, / What a loafer) or *boy* and some word that rhymes with *boy*.

LEFT THEN RIGHT, HEEL THEN TOE

I hiked along Superior's shore,
Weary feet on forest floor.
The trail was sixteen miles long.
I hiked and hummed a simple song:
"Eleven miles, five to go.
Left then right, heel then toe.
Five short miles left to go."

The world I'd left was far behind.
City things had left my mind.
No cars, no phones, no daily mail,
Just trusted boots against the trail.
"Left then right, heel then toe.
Five short miles left to go."

Fallen trees were all around.
Summer winds had pushed them down.
"Left then right, heel then toe.
Five short miles left to go.
Five short miles left to go."

The noise I heard stopped me short.
A heavy sound, a startled snort.
My head snapped up and to the right.
There he stood, a fearful sight.
A bear surprised upon his tree,
His nap destroyed by noisy me.

My life depended on his whim.
To live or die was up to him.
He turned and ran, afraid as I.
Why afraid? I don't know why.

I'd like to hike that trail once more,
Along the Lake Superior shore,
Feel unafraid in that sweet chore.
But there a black bear waits, I know,
For the sound of heel then toe.

About the Poem

This poem tells a true story. The trail was Lake Superior Trail in the Porcupine Mountains Wilderness State Park on Lake Superior near Ontonagon, Michigan. The following information about bears in the park is provided to hikers and campers by the park rangers from the Parks Division of the Michigan Department of Natural Resources, Lansing, Michigan.

CAUTION:

Misconceptions exist about wildlife in state parks, especially about bears. The Smokey Bear image has led some park visitors to believe that bears are friendly pets, while actually black bears can be dangerous! Garbage cans, food coolers, backpacks, even a sleeping bag, if it smells like food are all potential targets for investigation by bears.

Some campground bears have been known to pry open a clean, empty cooler, apparently using visual clues in recognizing it as a possible source of food.

A 200 pound bear can crawl through an opening a child would have trouble getting through and can easily tear out a car window left open only 1/2 inch.

While a bear looks big and clumsy, don't engage him in a foot race unless you can run about 35 miles an hour.

How can you avoid bear problems? The basis of the problem is food. Try to keep food, garbage, and odors from tempting bears. Keep your food in odor-tight containers in the trunk of the car with windows rolled up. Wash up dishes immediately after use. Backpackers should take special precautions to suspend food between two trees at least 10 feet high. If you can reach it easily, so can a bear.

Feeding a bear causes it to lose its fear of humans, to become a destructive nuisance, and eventually it may need to be destroyed.

Instructional Objectives

1. Students will recall narrative details.
2. Students will practice map-reading skills.
3. Students will practice research skills.
4. Students will engage in creative writing.
5. Students will present an original dramatic production.

Instructional Activities

1. Read "About the Poem" to the students to prepare them for their reading of the poem and to get them interested. It is possible that some children have experienced the fear of seeing a bear while camping. If so, let them share their experience with the class.
2. Have the students read the poem silently and take the following test:
   a. The trail was _____ miles long.
      (a) 5   (b) 12   (c) 16
   b. The hiker had already walked _____ miles.
      (a) 3   (b) 5   (c) 11
   c. The hiker was feeling
      (a) tired   (b) fresh
   d. The hiker had managed to forget
      (a) the wind   (b) city things   (c) warnings from the rangers
   e. The bear
      (a) growled   (b) snarled   (c) snorted
   f. The bear had been
      (a) sleeping on a tree
      (b) eating in the bushes
      (c) waiting for the hiker behind a tree
   g. The bear
      (a) charged   (b) ignored the hiker   (c) ran away
   h. The trail was on the shore of
      (a) Lake Superior   (b) Lake Michigan   (c) Big Bear Lake
3. Have the students locate the Porcupine Mountains on a map.
4. Assign three students to do some library research on black bears, Lake Superior, and the Porcupine Mountains. Have each report his or her findings to the class.
5. Divide the students into groups of three. Have each group prepare and present a mock radio interview. One student can introduce the program and deliver an original commercial, another can be the interviewer, and another can be the hiker.

WE'VE BEEN SO CLOSE

What can I say, We've been so close
I hate to see us end.
What a shame that you must be
My temporary friend.

Oh, my, the secrets we have shared,
That neither of us told.
Think back upon those years of ours.
Great Scott, I too am old.

Do you recall that summer day
I walked into the ocean
And let the waves unsand my legs,
With brash and splashing motion?

I tossed you far from me that day
To keep you from the wet.
I see you don't remember that,
But I shall not forget.

You've carried much that's dear to me,
While I have carried you.
It's hard to think that now, my friend,
We finally are through.

I'll take it now. It's mine, you know.
Can't trust you anymore.
You're old and torn, you can't recall
That walk along the shore.

About the Poem

I wrote this poem in a poetry-writing class I took in the English Department at the University of Wisconsin. The assignment was to write a riddle poem.

Instructional Objectives

1. Students will use context clues to identify the subject of the poem.
2. Students will identify instances of personification.

Instructional Activities

1. Tell the students that this is a riddle poem. Have them listen as you read for clues to the subject of the poem. Do not allow them to share their guesses until they have read the poem silently, decided upon the subject, and identified clues to support their decisions. Then ask them to tell their decision and explain it. Finally, tell them the author's subject was an old wallet.
2. Explain personification and have the students find examples of it in the poem.

MY DREAMS

Sometimes my dreams are very merry;
Other times they're very scary.
I've danced at balls with queens and kings,
Been chased and caught by monstrous things.

Where am I when I'm asleep?
I know my body's snuggled deep
Beneath the covers on my bed.
But where's the inside of my head?

Do my thoughts go out walking
When I stop my daytime talking?
Do they visit strange new places?
See different lands and different faces?

I think that they don't stay at home,
For in my dreams I often roam
Through areas unknown to me—
I've climbed a mountain, sailed a sea.

I never dream that I'm asleep,
Under covers snuggled deep.
I know my dreams are in my head,
But does my head stay in my bed?

About the Poem

The ancient Greeks believed that when people dreamed, their souls left their bodies and travelled to wherever they were dreaming about. I tried to capture that idea in this poem.

Instructional Objectives

1. Students will read to discover the central question asked in the poem.
2. Students will discuss their dreams and their notions of what happens when people dream.
3. Students will write a personal essay.
4. Students will list synonyms and antonyms for the word *merry*.

Instructional Activities

1. Tell the students to read the poem silently to discover and put into their own words the main question the poet is asking. Let them share their responses.
2. Divide the students into groups of four or five. Let them describe dreams they have had and explain their notions of what causes dreams and what happens when people dream. Assign each group to write a definition of the word *dream*. Have them compare their definitions with a dictionary definition.
3. Assign each student to write a personal essay on one of the following topics:

   A Dream I Would Like to Have
   A Dream I Hope I Never Have

   Let them read their essays orally to the class.
4. Have the students list words that are synonyms and antonyms for the word *merry*.

ANGRY WORDS

The words were sharp and stung my ear.
What right had he to make me hear,
"You're old and mean. You're bad and dumb."
What cause to clench his fist on thumb?

Somewhat stunned I stood and heard
My spirit sigh with each harsh word.
Such anger on a child's tongue,
Such anger in a head so young.

But then his voice was not alone.
The words he spoke were once my own.
Another voice, my own, I heard,
Spitting, piling word on word.

These hurtful words which stung my ear
I once had made my father hear.
The words which now were such a bother
I once had said to my own father.

About the Poem

I guess all children become angry with their parents occasionally. When they do, they often say things they later wish they had not said. Whether we are on the giving or the receiving end of angry words makes a big difference.

Instructional Objectives

1. Students will make inferences.
2. Students will identify descriptive words and phrases.
3. Students will identify figurative language.
4. Students will identify the exact words of the speaker.
5. Students will write an autobiographical description.

Instructional Activities

1. Tell the students to identify the relationship between the two characters as they read the poem silently. Then have them specify the clues that helped them make the inference.
2. Have the students pick out all the words and word phrases that support the title of the poem.
3. Explain what figurative language is. Have the students supply examples of figurative language from their own experience. Then have them identify figurative language in the poem.
4. Have the students identify the exact words spoken by the boy. Ask them how they knew.
5. Assign the students to write an autobiographical description of a time in their lives when they were very angry.

WHICH WAY TO THE BEACH?

For fifty-one weeks I save all my money
To go to an island that's sandy and sunny,
So I can swim in lovely blue sea.
No other delight's so delightful to me.

But I do get annoyed, yet find it quite funny
That while I'm spending all of my money,
Doing my best to make dollars reach,
The people who live there don't use the beach.

GEESE IN THE SKY

Geese flying south,
I'd watch if I could,
But with geese flying south
I'd better chop wood.

About the Poem

The Caribbean islands are my favorite vacation places. I especially enjoy swimming in the sea and walking along the beaches. It is interesting to me that the inhabitants do not seem to appreciate the sea or their beaches as much as I do.

Instructional Objectives

1. Students will read to infer the main idea.
2. Students will express their inference in a complete sentence.

Instructional Activity

Tell the students to read to discover the main idea in the poem. Then tell them to express the main idea in one complete sentence.

About the Poem

One fall morning I was splitting logs behind my cabin when I heard a flock of Canadian geese flying south in a huge V. They flew very low over the cabin and landed on the lake about fifty yards away from me. I wanted to stop cutting firewood and watch them, but I knew that geese flying south are always being chased by winter.

Instructional Objective

Students will infer main idea.

Instructional Activity

Read the poem to the students and ask them the following question:

Why doesn't the poet stop his work and watch the geese?

Then read them "About the Poem."

WHILE MOWING THE LAWN

A rustling sound, a small commotion
In the grass. I have a notion
It's a grass snake on its way.
To where or why I cannot say,
For I can't tell a grass snake's plan.
I only know the plans of man.
I've lived so long in city places,
Making money, reading faces,
That I've lost touch with things like snakes,
And deer and squirrels and bass in lakes.
A supermarket fills my needs.
I don't hunt game; I don't plant seeds.
I'm on a bridge that's getting longer;
My sense of loss is growing stronger.
I'm lonely for the wild, I guess.
Why else to write a poem like this?

About the Poem

I wrote this poem for all of my friends who have lost touch with nature. They have trapped themselves in the city and cannot seem to find an escape hatch.

Instructional Objectives

1. Students will use punctuation marks to read orally with good expression.
2. Students will become acquainted with advertisements for vacation retreats.
3. Students will write creatively.

Instructional Activities

1. Read the students "About the Poem" to prepare them for the message, which is somewhat adult.
2. Tell them to read the poem silently several times, paying close attention to punctuation marks. Then ask for volunteers to read the poem orally as they think the author might read it.
3. Show the students some newspaper advertisements for get-away-from-the-city vacations. Have them notice the use of vivid words and phrases. Then divide the students into groups of three and have each group create an advertisement that would appeal to the speaker in the poem.

OUTSIDE MY TENT

Outside my tent I hear something pawing,
Clawing and gnawing, hungrily mawing.
Maybe it's friendly, a friendly old deer,
Hungry or curious? I've nothing to fear
From a deer in search of a midnight snack
Who found the sandwich left in my pack.

Outside my tent I still hear it pawing,
Clawing and gnawing, stealthily mawing.
But now it sounds smaller. A hungry raccoon
Searching for food by the light of the moon?
Raccoons don't hurt people. No need now to fear.
I'm sure it's a raccoon—or maybe that deer.

Outside my tent that creature's still pawing,
Clawing and gnawing, greedily mawing.
What's that I smell? A skunk on the loose?
Oh how could I ever have been such a goose
As to trade my bed for this tent under trees,
To lie here all worried, sniffing the breeze?

Outside my tent the thing won't stop pawing,
Clawing and gnawing, ferociously mawing.
Now it sounds huge. It must be a bear,
Hungry and mean and ready to tear
Me to pieces before I can flee.
Oh, please! Someone, anyone, come rescue me.

Outside my tent no end to the pawing,
Clawing and gnawing, persistent, mawing.
I cannot stay here. I must look and see
The creature that may make a supper of me.
Bear or deer, raccoon or skunk—
I see it! Good grief—it's a tiny chipmunk.

About the Poem

On an automobile trip to Nova Scotia, Canada, I tented one night at North Bay, Ontario. My campsite was right on the bank of North Bay. During the night I awakened to a sound I had never heard before. Some creature was chewing and scratching outside my tent. I thought that if I lay quietly *it* would tire of my campsite and leave. *It* did not. After thirty minutes or so I had convinced myself it was a bear, and decided to scare it away with noise and a bright light. Accordingly I started shouting and stuck my bright flashlight out the door of my tent, right into the bright eyes of a startled chipmunk chewing on a hazel nut.

Instructional Objectives

1. Students will make predictions based on context clues.
2. Students will use context clues to define words.
3. Students will write and present an original dialogue based on the poem.

Instructional Activities

1. Project the poem on an overhead projector one stanza at a time. Give the students time to read each stanza, then call on a volunteer to read it orally. After each stanza is read orally ask the students to guess what is outside the tent. For the final stanza, disclose all but the last line.
2. Ask the students to define the words *mawing* and *persistent* using context clues. Explain that the verb *mawing* is derived from the noun *maw*. It is a made-up word.
3. Read the students "About the Poem." Then divide them into pairs. Assign each pair to write a dialogue between two tenters who hear a noise outside their tent. Tell the pairs to be guided by the poem, but to create any kind of ending they like. Have them present their dramatizations to the class.

TO SOCIETY'S LITTLE WORKS OF ART

To seldom-praised necessities,
Like faucets, nails, and front door _____.
I offer our apologies.

We simply never pause to think
About the beauty of a sink.
And no one ever gives a speech
To honor common, household _____.

Oh what a pity, sad but true,
No songs are sung in praise of glue;
No poems immortalizing cans,
Or forks or spoons or frying _____.

Now who has ever heard applause
For the sleigh of _____ _____ ?
No flags are flown for hard cement;
To dental _____ no knees are bent.

No parade goes marching by
Heralding the railroad _____.
Trumpets blare, but not for patches;
No bonfire's lit in praise of _____.

To you who serve us night and day,
From all of us I want to say,
You've earned a big "Hip, hip."
What's that you say? The car won't start?
Our radio just fell apart?
There are no teeth left in my comb?
I think I'd better end this poem.

About the Poem

This is a just-for-fun poem. However, I do think we take many things that make our lives better and easier for granted.

Instructional Objectives

1. Students will use context clues to replace deleted words.
2. Students will explain the title of the poem.
3. Students will read orally with good expression.
4. Students will make lists and compare them.
5. Students will write creatively.

Instructional Activities

1. Give the students the poem with the deletions. Have them replace the words and compare their replacements (keys, bleach, pans, Santa Claus, floss, tie, matches).
2. Ask for volunteers to explain why the title the poet gave to the poem is or is not a good one.
3. Assign one stanza to each of six students. Give them a minute to practice and then have them read the stanzas in sequence.
4. Have each student make a list of items other than those in the poem that could have been included in the poem. Let them compare their lists.
5. Assign the students to select one of "society's little works of art" and write an essay from the point of view of that item. Have them share their products.

KATIE THE GREAT

Once each day I like to be
Anything that pleases me.
"Here's my card, 'Katie Jean,
The Greatest Kid You've Ever Seen.'"

Watch me dance across this stage,
All America's latest rage.
This beautiful, graceful, dancing lady.
"Bravo, Bravo, Ballerina Katie!"

With Martians I have often fought
As fearless Katie Astronaut.
"My dear, I found the neatest place
While out exploring outer space."

Or sometimes I'm a movie star,
With furs and jewels and red sports car.
"Oh, my! We'll have to stand in line
To see this latest film of mine."

Most pilots wouldn't even try,
But I can tame the wildest sky.
"Clear the runway! Ready, men?
I'm going to land this DC-10."

To the poor I've given millions.
Perhaps I've even given trillions.
"Here's a check. It's all for you.
Build a hospital or two."

"You say a lion's broken loose?
Where's my gun? I'll cook his goose."
Lions, tigers, bears, and stuff
Better scram. This Katie's tough.

My clothes are all the latest fashion.
Dressing right for me's a passion.
See this contract in my hand?
Richest model in the land.

Every night I like to pause
And think a round of loud applause
Through the night all dark and deep,
Just before I fall asleep.

About the Poem

Everybody likes to daydream. Some of us like to daydream at night, to help us fall asleep. Katie the Great never has any trouble thinking of good things to dream about.

Instructional Objectives

1. Students will engage in mental imagery.
2. Students will read orally with good expression.
3. Students will give an oral description.
4. Students will write a descriptive essay.

Instructional Activities

1. Read the students "About the Poem" to arouse their interest.
2. Tell the students to read the poem silently, trying to get a mental picture of a four- or five-year-old girl posing for each stanza (for example, What is her posture? What is she wearing? How does she speak?). Then have volunteers describe their mental pictures and read the stanzas as they think Katie would say them.
3. Assign the students to write a description of their favorite daydream(s).

FIRST MONDAY IN APRIL

First Monday in April, clear 'cross the nation,
All children in school declared a vacation.
Instead of doing their spelling and stuff,
They stood up and shouted, "We've worked quite enough!"

"For years now we've toiled with paper and pen.
We now declare never to do that again.
We're going to start a new kind of school,
Where fun and games and tricks are the rule."

Their teachers were speechless, shocked to the core.
They never had seen this behavior before.
They watched as kids wrestled and played catch with books,
Completely ignoring their teachers' stern looks.

"Stop this right now," their teachers all pleaded,
But not even one of the school children heeded
The pleas of their teachers. They fell on deaf ears,
And were answered only with rudeness and jeers.

"Well," said the teachers, "there's nothing to do,
But join in these games and have some fun, too."
So much to the children's surprise and chagrin,
All over the country teachers joined in.

They threw paper airplanes clear cross the room,
And drummed on wastebaskets—Perdinkel, Perboom!
Pieces of chalk they rolled down the aisles.
Drew faces with frowns instead of with smiles.

They spun the globe 'till it made the kids dizzy.
When the children cried, "Teach!" they said, "We're too busy
Having ourselves a ball, can't you see?
Come on! Let's all dance, Ta-Ra-Whoop-Dee-Dee."

(Continued on page 140)

They pounded erasers under kids' noses,
And sat on their desks in funny, clown poses;
Scribbled on maps, on blackboards, on pages;
Even let gerbils out of their cages.

The children then said, "Please stop all these tricks.
We really wish you would not try to mix
Being teachers with mischievous fun.
The two together just cannot be done."

"What, what?" said the teachers, "what's all this fuss?
We like your new school. It's super for us
Not to plan lessons, correct all those papers.
We're ready and willing to keep up these capers."

The children were worried and looked kind of sick.
Not one of them wanted to play one more trick.
"We wish," said the children, "that you'd kindly lead
Us back to our old ways." The teachers agreed.

The school children learned a lesson that day:
Sometimes work can be more fun than play.
They also learned that it's really no kick
To be on the other end of a trick.

About the Poem

I wrote this poem on a warm, sunny Monday morning in April. I was visiting an elementary school. As I walked across the playground, I heard a teacher say to about forty students having recess, "Time to go in." One boy yelled, "Let's take a vote. See how many want to go in and how many want to stay here all day." About forty voices shouted, "Stay here!"

Instructional Objectives

1. Students will listen to recall details.
2. Students will state the moral in a complete sentence.
3. Students will use context clues to define words.
4. Students will attend to punctuation marks while reading orally.
5. Students will create a different ending and present it orally.
6. Students will write a mock newspaper story.

Instructional Activities

1. Before reading the poem aloud, instruct the students to attend to the specifics of the students' behavior and the teachers' behavior. Then read the poem and ask the students to recall as many things the students and teachers did to annoy each other as they can.
2. Have the students write the moral of the poem in one complete sentence. Have them read their sentences.
3. Write the following words on the chalkboard: toiled, jeers, chagrin, gerbils, capers. Then ask the students to explain how context clues help them to define each.
4. Assign stanzas to individual students. Tell them to prepare to read orally using punctuation marks as guides. Have the other students listen to see if the readers used the punctuation marks correctly.
5. Divide the students into pairs. Assign each pair to create a different ending for the poem. Have the pairs present their description orally. The ending need not be in poetic form.
6. Have each student choose the ending he or she likes best and write a newspaper report of the incident. Have them read their products orally.

Index